HEALING THE HURT CHILD INSIDE

About the Author

Deirdre Brady is a teacher with the Tipperary Education and Training Board and a Reiki Practitioner. She facilitates workshops throughout Ireland, mostly in personal development and mindfulness.

HEALING THE HURT CHILD INSIDE

A Journey of Abuse, Recovery and Forgiveness

Deirdre Brady

The Liffey Press

Published by
The Liffey Press Ltd
Raheny Shopping Centre, Second Floor
Raheny, Dublin 5, Ireland
www.theliffeypress.com

A catalogue record of this book is
available from the British Library.

ISBN 978-1-908308-90-0

Printed in Spain by GraphyCems.

Contents

Foreword, Dr Philip Moore   *vii*

PART 1
A GIRL CALLED DEIRDRE

Introduction   3

Chapter 1
Through the Eyes of a Child:
My Childhood as I Remember It   7

Chapter 2
Through the Eyes of an Adult Child   29

Chapter 3
Growing Up for Real   69

Chapter 4
Moving On   116

Chapter 5
The Pot of Gold   141

PART 2
LESSONS LEARNED

Chapter 6
Avoiding Pain and Finding Courage   165

Chapter 7
Denial, Addiction and the Cycle of Abuse   170

Chapter 8
The Armour that Is Anger   176

Chapter 9
Guilt and Shame   183

Chapter 10
Letting the Tears Fall   188

Chapter 11
The Grief of a Lost Childhood   192

Chapter 12
Being Empty and Still Again   197

Chapter 13
Self-love and Acceptance   202

Chapter 14
Forgiveness and the Cycle of Healing   214

Chapter 15
Practicing Mindfulness and Positivity   221

Chapter 16
Sugar and Spice – Self-belief and the Joy of Life!   228

Afterword
We Need a Better Understanding of Child
    Sexual Abuse   233

List of Counselling Services   240

Foreword

Dr Philip Moore

Registered Clinical Psychologist (Reg. Clin. Psychol. Ps.S.I.)

Deirdre's story is a love story. Yes it is also about childhood abuse and trauma, but above all it is inspiring in how it shows how love shines through to bring light in the darkness. Deirdre writes of a seeing a 'kaleidoscopic sky', but for me Deirdre herself is the kaleidoscope. Her love is the light that illuminates the different coloured broken bits of glass, beads and gems that form the different parts of her life – abuse, addiction, emotional neglect, hope, compassion and resilience. All of these co-exist and the light of her love is reflected on them so what we begin to see is a beautiful image emerging. Without the light of love the darkness prevents us from seeing the beauty that is already there. With the light and with a twist or turn, while all the parts remain the same, the image becomes transformed. In her story, Deirdre acknowledges that some of her life's precious turns happened in counselling, while in nature, experiencing Reiki, practicing mindfulness and with the support and love of friends. Deirdre gives us hope that we can continue to make our own twists in life and in these turns, experience moments of real transformation. This is encouraging for both those who have experienced childhood trauma and for those who are dedicated to helping and supporting them.

It takes enormous courage to battle the demons that can be both outside and, indeed, inside ourselves when we have experienced the traumas of abuse and addiction in our family. Deirdre, as we see, has courage in spades! This is not only seen through her grit and determination in dealing with much adversity in her life, but also in her then going on to write about it. We are privileged that she shares her story with us with such openness and honesty. This is such an act of generosity and love. The experience of childhood abuse can create isolation, loneliness, secrecy and shame. Exposing or uncovering it is an enormous challenge, understandably, far beyond what many can do. Deirdre's telling of her story can help others to realise that they are not alone, that others have had similar experiences and that it is indeed possible to prevail. Deirdre's positive energy charged through and that surely is an inspiration for those who may have yet to do battle or those who are still lost in battle. She is a modern day Irish heroine!

This book is important because it not only lifts the rock under which familial abuses have been lurking, it also exposes what can happen within families when someone in the system is brave enough to point them out. Others do not always want to see what is hidden in the shadows and may continue to shut their eyes, minimise or deny. The rock is shame and in many ways Irish society has experienced what could be called a collective shame in relation to childhood abuse, especially familial abuse.

In recent times much has been written, and rightly so, about the horrific abuses that have occurred within state-run institutions and the church but there is also abuse taking place in families that has had much less attention. Deirdre's book addresses this. As a society we were all shocked to read and listen to the stories of those abuses in institutional care. It is equally, if not more, shocking to read of abuse taking place within families. We cannot continue to turn away from the realities of familial abuse, though some may even be tempted to replace the rock. This is no longer an option.

There are still some nettles we as a society need to grasp. We do need to address the secrecy and shame within families as abuse thrives in secrecy. Members of families need to be open to listening without judging and shaming when abuse in disclosed and to help their family member access the necessary services and supports available. We need to expand and develop our over-stretched and under-resourced child protection services for the sake of our children of today. We also need to encourage more and more adults to come forward with their stories and disclose/report their abuse with the confidence that they will be believed, understood and supported. We also need to provide treatment services for perpetrators of sexual abuse to prevent further abuse.

Now we know so much about the impact of childhood abuse and trauma on the child and the adult into whom that child grows. Neuroscience has helped us to understand the brain's response to trauma and psychological research has much to inform us about the process of supporting and facilitating change for those who have experienced abuse as children. The impacts of abuse and trauma can vary from person to person. Some people need to tell their story and have it witnessed by another person as they may have never spoken of their past abuse before. Some need to express their emotions, grief and loss and find release. Some may experience symptoms of post-traumatic stress disorder (PTSD) such as flashbacks, nightmares and dissociation. Past trauma can be triggered by all sorts of everyday experiences and the person might not be able to make any sense of what is happening to them. They might even feel that they are going 'crazy' as they are overwhelmed and their reactions do not make logical sense. Counselling and psychotherapy can help with all of the above and more. Increasing self-awareness, developing skills in stabilising, containing and regulating emotions, processing memories, 'moving on'.

For anyone considering meeting with a counsellor/therapist it is certainly worth checking that they are accredited with a professional body. In addition, it is important that they have experience in working with trauma as this is an area that requires expertise. Services available and the professional bodies governing best practice in counselling/psychotherapy are listed at the end of the book.

My own professional life's work as a clinical psychologist and psychotherapist has been dedicated to helping adults who have experienced childhood trauma in the form of abuse and/or neglect. Counselling and psychotherapy can be of huge help, and in the service in which I work we have the evidence from thousands of adults across the country who have been able to transform their sense of self and the lives they live. The process of healing and recovery can be a delicate one at times, but when a person is ready and they feel safe enough to trust another, then the healing can truly begin. Making a first call, attending that first meeting, reaching out, are all important steps – like planting seeds that make their fragile attempts to grow towards the light and which ultimately can bloom and flourish. Understandably, this can feel like taking a big risk. Of course it does. Life experiences have taught that others have hurt, abused, neglected so it is only natural to be cautious. This is where the courage comes in, taking those tentative steps to risk connection both with self and with another.

Engaging in a counselling/psychotherapy process both the client and the counsellor/therapist meet at agreed regular frequency and time. The counsellor/therapist is there with the intention of meetings the client's needs and will always act in the client's best interests. The counsellor/therapist does not sit in judgement but is there to help increase understanding and insight. The therapeutic relationship allows for the client to experience a sense of safety with another and the boundaries of the therapeutic process can enhance this. Trust can then be built from this solid foundation. This in itself can be reparative. The counsellor/therapist will work through the client's issues at a pace that is controlled by the client. Empowering the client to recognise and honour their limits is a crucial aspect of counselling/psychotherapy. The counsellor/therapist will be attuned to the client's needs and can help to clarify these even when the client might be unaware of them as they remain unconscious. Gently encouraging the client to move outside their comfort zones may also be part of the therapeutic process. The care, compassion and empathy that the counsellor/therapist has for the client can eventually become internalised by the client and can co-exist or even replace the internal bully or critic or abuser who is so often dominant in people who have experienced childhood abuse. A new, unfamiliar voice can begin to be heard, listened to and appreciated.

In my own experience of working therapeutically with clients, I have come to realise that sometimes words are not enough. When providing trauma therapy, the 'talking therapies' sometimes need to be enhanced with more creative approaches. Body work can be hugely important in healing trauma. Sometimes the body remembers what the conscious mind does not. Paying attention to posture, playing with movements and gestures, generating sound that is not word-based language can all bring healing. The client may also be invited to engage in creative experiential opportunities that can promote imaginative and intuitive right-brain activities such as art and image making, writing and poetry, working with metaphor and story. Self-discovery, self-acceptance and self-love can all emerge from these processes.

From the time I have spent with those who have experienced childhood trauma, I have come to believe in an inner resource, in all of us. Some call this psyche, some call it soul. For Deirdre, she calls it God, Light, Love. Whatever we call it, it is there, can be accessed and can be an infinite source of treasure. Deirdre's story tells us that when you do access it, life can become rich in ways that could not have been imagined. The invitation to new frontiers...

May my mind come alive today
To the invisible geography
That invites me to new frontiers,
To break the dead shell of yesterdays,
To risk being disturbed and changed.

May I have the courage today
To live the life that I would love,
To postpone my dreams no longer,
But do at last what I came here for
And waste my heart on fear no more

– John O'Donohue, 'Benedictus'

*I would like to dedicate this book to forgiveness
and to love, to my family and everyone
who have helped me along the way,
especially Eileen Heneghan:
my light-house,
who always believed in me –
even when I didn't!
Thank you all.*

In memory of my mother, Elizabeth Morris Brady.

Part 1

A Girl Called Deirdre

Introduction

This book is about understanding and healing the hurt caused by an unhappy childhood, dealing with issues that shaped my own childhood including child sexual abuse, alcoholism and emotional neglect. I didn't want to just write a book about love and positivity without writing about what life is like without these things. I want readers to relate to me and my story, so that they don't feel alone, so that they can see that anything is possible. If I could recover from a childhood like I had, I believe that anyone can. Some people have experienced much more trauma than I have, and some have had less, but we can all heal and I hope this book can help do just that.

I also want to help people become more mindful of not judging others. We are all only as good as the foundations that we have holding us up. We learn about life from the people we grow up with and it's important to remember that all our life experiences are different. Some have been lucky to grow up in a secure, loving home and learn positive lessons about life, relationships, money, trust, love and so on. They learn to make choices based on self-love and respect and they feel supported and valued in their lives. Others, like me, haven't been so lucky and when someone doesn't love or respect themselves, their choices in life will always reflect that. Sometimes, we get the opportunity to start over and build a new foundation, a new life – and thankfully I did, but even that requires courage and a real desire to change. If someone doesn't believe enough in themselves or in something better, they may never find the tools or the support to change their own lives, no matter how unhappy they may be.

This is my story and I hope that it can help to heal and inspire others – this is my reason for writing it. My own father abused me when I was a young child between the ages of three and six approximately. I also witnessed him sexually assault another child, while in my company. He went on to become an angry and verbally abusive alcoholic throughout my teenage years. My oldest brother molested me (another word for child sexual abuse), over a period of about a year, when I was around twelve. My mother was co-dependent and I learned, through the process of psychotherapy, that my family were classically dysfunctional, with each one taking on a different role. This book is an attempt to help understand the damage that can be done to a child who has experienced sexual abuse and addiction within the family and, more importantly, how to heal that child, because I was that child.

I would describe my family of origin as a broken one, with little trust and very little closeness. I believe that the abuse that my father suffered as a child created his own confused sexuality and perverse desires. I also believe that he drank to numb the feelings of guilt or shame that he had. This and his inability to love himself, overwhelmed by feeling of self-loathing and shame brought about his addiction to alcohol. I will never understand how or why my father did what he did to me and to other young girls: how he could live with himself after what he did and how he could continue to do it. Nor will I understand why my brother chose to do what he did – the brother that I idolised so much growing up. I wonder if they had known the hurt and pain that they were to cause, whether they would have still behaved the way they did and acted on their selfish, perverse sexual desires. I don't know the answers to these questions and I have accepted that, just as I have accepted all the answers that I have found.

I am the youngest in my family and there are twenty-nine years between us all. I have changed my siblings' names, as per their request. I talk about my eldest brother Alan in this story, as his actions had a direct and personal impact on my life. Alan lives in America and has done for many years. I will also talk of my sister Marie, only in relation to me and my story as her life is her own to discuss. Although she lives in America, we have become closer as the years have passed and have much in common. I love her dearly. I have other brothers, Jack and Paul, who I do not have much contact with. I won't be discussing them or their lives to protect their privacy. Suffice to say that all of us were deeply affected by our childhoods. My brothers had the added difficulty of having a father and role model who was a very damaged, self-absorbed man, unable to have any real or healthy relationship with anyone, least of all himself.

We cannot change our family of origin or the childhood experience that is unique to each of us. We can, however, heal from our past and if we want to have healthy relationships and/or a healthy and happy family of our own, it is imperative that we do so. What we don't heal, we carry with us and this will define our adult life in one way or another. Healing the hurt child is about healing the angry, hurt, confused child within us and learning to love and value ourselves in the process.

Part 1 of this book is my own personal experience as I remember it and how my childhood shaped my adult life. I also tell how I repaired the damage, learned how to live my own life and began to heal my pain. Part 2 is about the process of healing and the lessons that I learned on my emotional journey. In an Afterword I discuss the issue of child abuse more generally and how as a society we have to start talking about it and understand it better.

Chapter 1

Through the Eyes of a Child:
My Childhood as I Remember It

*'Sugar and spice and all things nice, that's what
little girls are made of. Slugs and snails and puppy
dog tails, that's what little boys are made of.'*

When I first heard this rhyme, I believed that I was
made from the latter, or worse. There was nothing
sweet or nice about me and that was for sure.

The first memory I have is shortly after arriving in our
new home in Skerries in North county Dublin. I am four years
old and this is our fifth home in four years. My parents, who
originally came from the southeast of the country, moved to
Kilkenny for ten years before a business venture brought my
father and the family to Dublin. I was born in Kilkenny and
have three older brothers and one sister. We first lived on the
southside of the city and we moved a few more times before I
found myself in Skerries in North County Dublin in the first
home that I remember.

I'm standing in the front garden of a semi-detached two story house in a large estate observing my new neighbourhood. It is a lovely, sunny summer's day. There is a green just a little way down from our house and there are some children playing there. The next moment, a very pretty girl about my age, with blond curly hair is standing on the other side of our driveway gate. She asks me if I will be her friend, with a big dimply smile and a halo of golden curls around her head. I happily agree and Sophie and I skip off together. Within minutes we're playing on the swings in her back garden and she's telling me all about her family and the adventures that she has with her dad and her sister Ann.

Sophie and I become best friends. We play games on the green with the other kids, we bait crabs in the estuary nearby and we start school together that September. My mother brings me to school on my first day and I am terrified. I don't want my mom to leave me there and I cry inconsolably. She tells me that she has forgotten to bring a banana for me to eat and she leaves to go to the shop, promising to come straight back. I sit by the window, watching and waiting for my mother. She doesn't come back until school is over. I am hurt and angry with her because she broke her promise. I like my teacher though and after a few weeks, I start to like school. My teacher's name is Mrs White and she is very kind. We play with Marla and make things with lollipop sticks and bricks and all sorts of games I have never played before.

I don't remember my own home at this point in my life nor have I any family memories. I can recall Sophie's house: her kitchen, living room, bedroom and even the smell of her home, but I can't remember anything of mine. I remember going to the shop on Saturday mornings with my brother

Paul, Ann and Sophie to get sweets. We would come out of Dan's corner shop, after parting with fifty pence each, with a bagful of sweets which we proceeded to eat all the way home: Bulls 'eyes, sherbet fizz, black jacks and jaw breakers – little morsels' of heaven.

I have only one other strong memory of this time and I carried it around like a dog with a bone for many years, before I eventually forgave my mom and let it go. It involved a trip to our nearest relatives, Aunt Katie and Uncle Des – Mom's sister and husband – who lived in County Kildare. They moved back to Ireland from England as my uncle had got a new job. Des was a public servant and Katie was a stay-at-home mom, just like mine. They had two daughters, Ellie and Sarah. Ellie, their youngest, was a few months younger than me and we got on very well together. We probably saw them once or twice a month, taking it in turns to make the trip from Dublin to Kildare.

I'm about six now. It is a Saturday morning and all of my family and I pile into Dad's car and drive to my aunt and uncle's house in Kildare. All except my oldest brother Alan – I don't know where he is. The rest of my family go off shopping, promising to return for me later that day. I play in the garden with my cousin, Ellie. At some point, my Aunty Katie calls me into the kitchen and tells me that the rest of my family have gone on their holidays to Spain for two weeks! When I get over the shock of it, I am hurt and confused. Why didn't they bring me? Why did they not tell me and why did they lie to me? Maybe it was my fault. Maybe I wasn't good enough...

I spend the time playing with my two cousins, Ellie and Sarah in their garden. They have a big grey and red metal rocking horse with springs on each corner that I play on a lot. I love horses and I pretend to be Eddie Macken, jumping a winning round in the RDS. My aunt and uncle are very kind. Aunty Katie cooks sausages for me nearly every day and makes me sweet milky coffee and toast most evenings. I love her sweet coffee; I'm not allowed to drink it at home. I get to stay up late too! Towards the end of the two weeks I feel lonely for my family and for my home. When they come to collect me, I feel angry and happy at the same time. They have brought me back presents – the first is a big horrible Spanish ornamental doll (which I hate as I've never liked dolls), and this one doesn't move or do anything, so what am I supposed to do with it? The second present is a red and white frilly, polka-dot dress, which I couldn't have disliked more. The third thing is a pair of castanets — finally something I like and can make noise with!

The doll sat on top of the bar (yes, there was a bar) in our sitting-room for years after, goading me in her red dress, as she did something resembling the can-can, reminding me of the holiday that I never went on.

Two years pass and I am eight years old, or thereabouts. I love horses more than anything, more than my family even (well, most of them anyway). I've been getting riding lessons at the local stables with my sister Marie and my brother Paul. We go most Saturday mornings and I look forward to it all week. We walk down in our wellies and I jump around excitedly, wondering if I'm going to be riding Rusty or Doormouse or maybe even Midnight. I'm hoping that Santa will bring me a pony for Christmas this year – I asked last year and he didn't bring me one. I guess I haven't been good enough. I've been getting into trouble a lot at school lately.

My mom is always telling me I'm 'as bold as brass', whatever that means, and I am cheeky to my teacher, Mr Burke, but that's because he's a horrible, mean little man. This is the second horrible year to have Mr Burke, as we had him in first class too. I miss our old teacher Mrs White and I don't like school anymore. In fact, I'm beginning to really hate school.

Mr Burke is small and stout (like the teapot), with lots of curly, black, afro-like hair that sits around his head like a motor-bike helmet. He has a big long ruler (he calls it a metre stick) and he walks around the classroom with it, using it like a walking stick. Sometimes he slaps us with it for talking or messing.

At the beginning of first class Mr Burke asked if anyone knew which letters were vowels. I put my hand up and when he picked me, I answered 'ahh, aye, ee, oh and ew'. Of course these were the vowel *sounds* that we had learned the year before, not the actual vowels, which in hindsight was quite clever for a six (and a half) year old. Mr Burke didn't think it was clever: he thought it was very funny and asked the class if maybe I thought I was a monkey and everybody laughed. The second time he ridiculed me was with the age-old question about the ton of feathers and the ton of coal, which one was heavier? What is a seven-year-old going to say? In hindsight, if I was in any doubt about Mr Burke's sadistic nature and whether my feelings were justified at the time, he really was setting me up for a fall this time and my hatred of him seemed righteous. He ridiculed me a few more times before I stopped putting my hand up when he asked a question and soon I was retorting with the same sarcasm and hatred that he so frequently liked to use. And so I began my school life as an angry and belligerent student.

My brother Jack teases me a lot too and I'm regularly told that I was left on the doorstep, or that I was adopted and that my real name was 'Way Way Wong' and I was from Hong Kong. He's mean to me and Mom never says anything to him, even when he makes me cry. I have found a hideout in the back of the downstairs closet. It smells of shoe polish and the hoover, but I like it because nobody knows I'm there – I can hide from the world.

I still like being outdoors best and my new favourite games are climbing trees and kiss-chasing, in that order. I'm faster than all the boys so I can choose who I want to catch me. It's usually Shane – he has lovely brown eyes, like our dog Max and brown curly hair and he's kind and has a lovely smile.

I dread going to my cousins' house now, not because of them, but because of Dad. Every time we visit them, Dad and Uncle Des go to the pub and when they come back Dad smells of whiskey and has a big red face. He brings sweets back for us, which he only ever gets when our cousins are around. In the car on the way home, my mom and dad shout a lot and my dad drives the car very fast and says he is going to crash and kill us all. His favourite threats involve driving into the next telegraph pole or driving over the cliff on the coast road. I believe him and am very frightened. I close my eyes, crouch down in the back-seat and say the *Hail Mary* to myself all the way home.

I have a lot of bad dreams lately too. There is one that I have over and over and it wakes me up every time. . . I am in a coffin and I have been buried alive! I am really scared and I scream and bang on the inside of the coffin lid, hoping someone will hear me. The inside of the coffin is dimly lit and I can just make out the red shiny fabric on the inside of the lid. It is hot and I can hardly breathe. I get so upset that I jump up out of my bed with my heart beating like a drum and my nightie stuck to my body with sweat.

I particularly hate Sunday nights; maybe it's because we go to late mass on Sunday – five thirty in the evening – and in the winter it's dark and cold. The priest always seems to be talking about sinning and hell and this worries me. I hate mass and I hate the dark, and I really hate having horrible nightmares!

I don't remember home-life at all and I don't remember Christmas time or birthdays or anything like that. I can vaguely remember what's going on in school, but I do remember my mom going to a parent-teacher meeting, because when she comes home from the meeting she tells me that I can't go horse riding anymore; Mr Burke said that it was interfering with my schoolwork. I think she's joking at first. *No*, she says, *Mr Burke said that no matter what he asked us to write about, that I always wrote about horses; either my riding lesson or being down at the stable, that it was all horses, horses and more horses and it was distracting me from my schoolwork.*

Well of course I wrote about horses because I loved them! Going horse-riding was my favourite past-time in the world by far! I lived for it and Mr Burke knew that. I can't believe that he could be so cruel and I can't believe that my mother would listen to anything that Mr Burke says, but she does and I can't go to my favourite place in the world and do the one thing that makes my life bearable. I hate my life. I hate my family and I hate Mr Burke. I didn't think he could hurt me this much, but I wasn't banking on something like this happening.

One day, Sophie and I are taking the shortcut down to the estuary when we notice a tent pitched in the rough grass behind the houses. A young man comes out and called us over. He's a bit scruffy and had long hair but he smiles and seems friendly, so we go over. He asks us if we want to see something really special – a tiny person that was so small that he could fit in a matchbox! We say that we would love to see it and so he brings us inside and shows us the matchbox with a tiny little man in it. He tells us that the little man is asleep, but that he can talk and play and do lots of fun things. Then the man tells us that we can have one too, only we'd have to do something to make the magic happen. We'd have to put his willy in our mouths and suck it until he says, and then a little person will magically grow in the empty matchbox he shows us. He asks Sophie to do it first and she said no. Then he asks me and I do it. I don't actually remember doing it, but I know I do it and the man gives me the matchbox and tells me not to open it until the next day and not to tell anybody either. We leave and Sophie says she has to go home. She looks worried and I know something is wrong. I go home too.

Only my sister Marie is at home, so I tell her what had happened and about the matchbox and the little person that is going to be my very own friend. Marie, who is fourteen at the time, is shouting at me now and asking me all sorts of questions. Then the phone rings and Sophie's mom is on the phone to my sister and they have called the police who are on the way. When the police call to the door, I know I've done something really bad. My stomach is churning and I feel so dirty and sick inside. My mother seems even more horrified when she returns with my father. He doesn't say anything at all. The police look for the man, but don't find him and in a few days the whole thing is forgotten.

Around this time, a Spanish couple called Norita and Lucas come to stay with us. They are friendly and kind and they stay in our house for a whole month. Norita is an artist and draws a lovely picture of me with the words 'For Deirdre, Very friendly'. Mom is always making me wear silly dresses and skirts with matching headbands or knickers. She parades me out in front of our guests. I don't like dresses anymore and I hate wearing them, but my mom is cross and quick to use the wooden spoon, so I do what I'm told! Mom is always busy and I wish she would play with me or talk to me, but she never does. Most of the time I feel very lonely at home.

We move house again, although I am still within walking distance of Sophie's house. I do love the village we live in and I've decided that the outdoors would be my home, whichever house we lived in. It's a lovely area and there are lots of fun places to go and games to play. There are lots of kids to play games with too. I love to be outside playing 'British Bulldogs, 1,2,3', or 'Red Rover' or 'Kick the Can.' I love playing down at the estuary too, or in Sophie's house. Her sister Ann is a year older than us. My brother and I start swimming lessons every Saturday morning with Sophie and Ann. Our dads take it in turns to bring us each week. Sophie and her sister don't like my dad, even though he buys sweets or ice cream for them. I can tell by how quiet they are. I still love horses and really miss going horse riding. My sister and brother stopped going too; I don't think we can afford it anymore.

My oldest brother Alan is getting married. I don't really like the lady he is going to marry. I love my big brother – he's always putting me up on his shoulders and swinging me around. He brings me for spins in his fast car and sometimes he buys me sweets or an ice pop. I like him way more than I like my dad. I don't want Alan to go to Galway and I worry that I might never see him again . . .

Time moves on, as it does, and I am ten years old now. We moved house again when I was nine and I never see Sophie now. We still live in Skerries, but now on the other side of the village. I have changed schools too and I'm in fourth class now. I don't go swimming any more either. I have made new friends, but when I first moved I missed my old estate and I missed Sophie too. We agreed to meet up again in secondary school, but I've already forgotten about that. I've long stopped kissing boys and now I mostly want to fight them. The good thing is there are lots of boys around to fight! The school that I'm going to now had been an all boys' school and we're the first class of mixed boys and girls. Fifth and sixth class are all boys and I'm always fighting them. I have rules though: I never fight anyone younger than me, I never fight girls and I never kick anyone in the head. I haven't lost a fight yet. I don't understand what gets into me; it's like a rage comes up from inside me and I lash out, hitting and kicking mercilessly. I don't stop until the other person is on the ground, pleading and surrendering, or running away (which is often the case). My new teacher Mr O'Carroll has his own anger issues and he broke our classroom door, throwing my friend Alison against it! He gets so angry that his face turns purple. Needless to say, I still hate school.

I can remember much more about my home life now, but none of it is good. I share a bedroom with my sister Marie, who doesn't talk to me much and she's moody too. My brothers have their own rooms. My Mom and Dad argue from the minute my Dad comes home from work and for most of the weekends too, until Dad goes to the pub. Sometimes he doesn't come home until really late and then there's a big row. I sit on the stairs and try to hear what they're saying; it's always about Dad's drinking or money, or both. I go back to bed wishing it could be different and dreaming of a dad that loved me, that would come home and sweep me up into his arms, kiss me and cuddle me and make me feel special.

I know Mom is unhappy and I wish I could make it better for her too. She rarely laughs or even smiles. She does tell me that she loves me sometimes, but she never spends any time with me. Dad smells of whiskey most of the time and I hate him. He comes in with a mean, ugly, sneering face and he's always looking for a row. I keep my head down mostly and out of the way as much as possible. He is always picking on my brothers and starting rows.

I have a new friend, Claire, who's in my class at school. We both love horses and we've started getting horse riding lessons every other week. I have to beg Mom for the money, but we work at the stables every day after school now too and get free lessons as payment. I really love every minute there and I live for Saturday mornings when we can spend hours there, helping out in the yard. Two brothers run the stables, Charlie and Dave, and they're very nice and fair with us. We water and feed the ponies and horses. We muck out the stables, sweep the yards and lead the beginners in the lessons. We get one or two lessons a week for helping out and it's great! I have a favourite pony, called Bobby, who is a naughty, but very handsome little bay stallion with a bushy black mane and tail and he's always getting into trouble in the lessons. He behaves himself for me though and sometimes, when he's being naughty (with someone else on board) and keeps refusing a jump, I have to get up on him and show him who's in charge. It makes me feel important and I love Bobby all the more for it. I hug him and kiss him in his stable and when I look into his big brown eyes, it's as if he can look right inside me and see things that nobody else knows – my deep dark secrets. It's hard to explain but I find it very reassuring knowing that he understands me and knows me in a way that nobody else does. The stables and Claire's house are the only places that I feel happy and relaxed.

I love going to Claire's after school and sometimes she asks me to sleep over at the weekend too. I love everything about her home and her family are so nice. Her mom, Mrs Drum, always seems to be calm and relaxed and is always baking, doing housework or sitting in the conservatory, reading or relaxing. Mr Drum works as an accountant and usually spends his weekends pottering around the garden. He cycles down to the pier to swim and sometimes we go with him, as they have an assortment of bicycles to choose from. Mr Drum is quite strict and serious, but he's also kind and is interested in everything and is always asking Claire and me questions. He annoys Claire sometimes, but I think he's great. He grows gooseberries and artichokes and even grapes. One Saturday morning, when things are getting worse at home and there's no money for me to go horse riding, Mr Drum, who sees that I am upset and disappointed, gives Claire the money for me to go too. His kindness gives me a warm feeling in my heart and a lump in my throat.

I dread going to Kildare, as Dad always gets very drunk when we go there now and the trip home is a nightmare. I still close my eyes most of the way home and pray. I know every turn in the road by heart and I reckon I'd be able to make the journey blindfolded if I had to. My sister has stopped coming with us, so it's just Mom, my brother and I who have to brave it.

One Saturday morning, I remember standing at the train station with my mother, waiting for the train to come and take us to Dublin. There had been a row at home and before I knew it, I was walking down to the station with my mother. It was such a novelty for me and to my surprise, a big shiny, green steam train, chugged impressively into the station and filled it with white steam. It was like something from a Disney film and the trip was just as magical, with the train gliding along like a living thing, like a giant green dragon with its very own heartbeat. It was my only time in a steam train and I'll never forget it, especially when it whistled ferociously as it approached each station. It was much nicer than the diesel trains that we sometimes took into Dublin and it was so much better than going anywhere with Dad.

I prefer when my cousins come over to see us. I like my cousin Ellie. We play games up in my room. We don't like dolls and when we get them, we rip off their arms and legs and cut all their hair off. We write on them with pens and gouge their eyes out. Then we usually drown them in the sink! Sometimes we play games with our 'private parts'. It started one time when I showed Ellie how to rub herself up and down against a cushion. I don't know when it started, but now I am always sticking things up inside myself and I show Ellie how to as well. I don't know why, because afterwards it makes me feel kind of sick inside, like I've done something bad.

Time pushes forward again and I am twelve years old. We still live in the same house in Sea View, which must be a record – more than two years in the same house! My oldest brother Alan is going to America. His marriage has broken up and he moved back in with us before deciding to go away with his friend Brian who has an uncle in California. When I was younger, I really liked my oldest brother; he had more time for me than my Dad and he was always laughing and joking. I always felt safe with him when I was younger too, even when he drove very fast in his yellow sports car with everyone looking at us passing. It was exciting and fun, but when he moved back home he was different.

He comes into my room now and tells me to lie on my bed. He says that he's going to give me a massage and gets me to lie on my belly. Then he lies on top of me and moves up and down on me, rubbing me and making grunting noises. I don't like it at all – it makes me feel dirty and ashamed, which is really confusing, as I don't understand what is happening. I know that it isn't right and I have found a place to hide from him. I climb up into the top of the built-in wardrobe in my room as often as I can when Alan's around. I like hiding in here; nobody can find me in my secret den. I take some spare pillows from the hot-press and a torch from Mom's drawer so I can read my comics. My sister Marie, who I still share a room with, works in Dublin city in an insurance company. I can relax when she comes home from work as Alan won't come near me then. One day Alan catches me off guard and I don't even hear him coming up the stairs. I start to feel the usual nausea when he comes in and my head feels like it is going to explode and I can hardly breathe under the weight of him and when he gets up, I so badly want to say something to him, but I can't.

Thankfully, just when I think I can't take any more, Alan leaves for America.

I miss Alan, which confuses me sometimes, because of what he did when he came into my bedroom. My mother misses him terribly and she doesn't seem to be coping very well. She's either cleaning the house obsessively or crying or shouting, and sometimes all three!

I have noticed changes in my body lately. I have begun to 'develop', as my mother calls it and I'm not impressed. Mom gives me a little booklet one day about the birds and the bees and I want to die! I want to be a boy, not a girl, turning into a stupid woman! I hate skirts and dresses. I never wear anything but jeans and sweatshirts (even if they are horrible brown ones my mom has picked out) and I'm certainly not going to wear a bra! I get my hair cut short now and sometimes I am mistaken for a boy, which I pretend doesn't bother me, but it really does. How complicated am I? My older sister has a perm in her hair now and she wears high-heeled boots with skirts and she wears dresses all the time. Mom loves Marie. She has always been so good and she's never cheeky like me. I'm always fighting with Mom and slamming doors. I'm always angry and Mom says I'm horrible and selfish and have a 'dirty rotten temper.'

The teenage years come all too quickly and before I know it, I'm fourteen. I managed to persuade Mom to let me go to a private secondary school in Dublin city because my friend Claire was going there. I knew we couldn't really afford it and I didn't think she would agree, but surprisingly she did. Marie is working and is helping out financially, so that might be why. There are seven of us in the same year that travel from Skerries every day and we've become great friends. They are my lifeline, these girls, and without them I don't know how I'd cope. They call me Dee and the name sticks forever more. Suzanne and Barbara live nearby and they call over most evenings during the week. Our house has a half-converted garage (since the time Alan moved back) where I spend most of my time. We call it 'the den.' I love music and we have quite a lot of albums, everything from Supertramp and Pink Floyd to David Bowie and the Stranglers. My friends and my music, but particularly my friends, keep me sane! Suzanne and I have started smoking – can't help it if we're cool! Claire and I slowly drifted away from the stables; we didn't have as much time in secondary school and I'd given up on the dream of owning my own pony.

My brother Jack has gone to the States now too. Alan offered him a job in the factory he was working in. I'm getting on better with my sister now and we chat sometimes when we're in bed at night. Dad is working as a sales rep, although I don't know how he keeps down a job or doesn't kill himself driving. He came close when he fell asleep while driving last year and crashed into a tree – anybody else would have died. Dad, with the proverbial luck of the Devil, managed to survive. He broke his leg and hip very badly and has to use a crutch all the time now, but he lived. I hate my Dad and can honestly say I wish he had died in that crash, and even though I know that sounds horrible it's the truth. He doesn't come home until late every night and he is always obnoxiously drunk. The weekends are worse because Mom usually spends the morning fighting with Dad over money and his drinking. Sometimes I get involved too, pleading with him not to go to the pub. Then he goes to the pub anyway, usually around lunchtime, which means he comes home really drunk and in foul form, looking for a fight with whoever is around. I stay in the den mostly, but sometimes he comes in, usually when my friends are there, sneering and scowling and slurring something incoherently. I get so embarrassed by him. When my friends go, and the door closes out behind them, I feel such desolation. I feel so alone and I often cry my heart out. Then I get angry and cut my arms and wrists, not deeply or anything, but just to hurt myself. I just feel so frustrated and angry and for some reason it just makes me feel better. I wish I could rip my arms apart, but I don't have the nerve.

Sweet sixteen I wish I was. I may be sixteen now and I would love to say that my life has got better, but it hasn't – it's even worse! Alan came home last Christmas and persuaded my sister to go back to the States with him. It's my mother's fault – Marie wouldn't have gone if Mom had let her move out when she wanted to. She was twenty-three, single and was still working at the insurance company in Dublin at the time. Two friends of hers from work were getting an apartment in the city centre and asked Marie to join them. She was so excited at having her independence (and getting away from our house of horrors), but Mom was having none of it. She said that Marie owed her for putting her through secretarial school and that she depended on her money every month: how would she pay for my school, for starters? Mom held firm and said Marie could leave when she got married and not before.

Desperation set in and Marie put up a fight, saying she was a grown woman and was entitled to get her own place. She even said that she could still contribute at home if she sold her car. It was the first time I had ever seen my sister really stand up to Mom, who was having none of it – she finally snapped and got into such a rage, saying, 'If you leave, you'll never set foot inside my door again – ever!' Well that was that and Marie remained trapped in our unhappy home until Alan came home and offered her a job. Mom could never refuse Alan.

For Marie, it was an escape, at least that's how I saw it. It was her only way out of our sinking ship of a family. We shared the same bedroom and we had really only become close in the last couple of years. Marie was quiet and she wasn't affectionate or cuddly either, but she was very protective and took her responsibilities as a sister very seriously. She could be very bubbly and funny too, and she made me feel very safe. Marie had a wine Citroen Diane and would give me a lift some mornings into school. We would bring a rug for our legs because the heater didn't work and Marie always brought a flask of coffee for the trip. We chatted and listened to 'Sunshine Radio' all the way into town. I loved travelling with my big sister into school and she dropped me at the door too, so I didn't have to walk up from the station. It was a great start to my day.

When Marie got ready to leave home, I just pretended that she wasn't going. It was working well for me until she was walking through the departure gates at Dublin Airport. I will never forget the pain that I felt that day. I was completely overwhelmed by the feelings of loss, sadness, hurt and sheer panic that I felt. For the first time that I could remember, I thought I was going to lose my sanity. When my friend Barbara called to my house later that same day, I became totally hysterical. I roared crying and I found it difficult to breathe. The pressure that I felt inside my head was so bad that I thought my head was going to explode. Barbara was there for me – my friends always were and I felt so lucky for that.

Things continue to get worse: Dad has another car accident, driving through a red light and straight under an articulated lorry. Only one broken bone this time – his arm – but he gets fired from his job this time, which is a real disaster. He's walking down to the nearest pub every day now and getting very drunk. I've had to go down a few times and help him home and it's so embarrassing! He is so horrible when he's drunk, which is most of the time now. The odd time that he's sober, he cries and is very pathetic. I hate him so much it frightens me. He's not giving Mom any money either and says he'd rather 'piss it against the wall' than give it to her. I've had to ring Alan from a call box a few times now to ask him to send over money.

Mom has become much more dependent on me since Marie left and not in a good way. It's as if her problems are my problems now. It makes me very angry sometimes because she has no interest in me or my life. She thinks I should put her first. When I challenge her or tell her something she doesn't want to hear, she gives me what I call 'the big chill', ignoring me completely for days, sometimes for weeks on end. She's so good at it too, being cold and cruel. I don't exist to her when I'm being frozen out. I could walk into a room, ask her a question and leave again, without her even looking up; it's as if I'm invisible. It makes me so angry and hurt and, to make things worse, she's always extra nice to my brother when she's angry with me and makes his favourite dinners and desserts. Mom uses him as an intermediary, saying things like, 'Tell your sister to do the dishes and clean up the kitchen.' I usually start slamming doors around the house because I know she can hear me and she can't give out to me when she's not talking to me. I have cried myself to sleep so many times. She won't break me though – I *will* speak my mind, no matter what the consequences are. When things between us are good, life is more bearable. She lets me stay off school when I ask her (usually when it's raining), saying she'd be glad of the company. We sometimes walk to the village to get some groceries, stopping at the local coffee shop for tea and cakes. I'm more often sorry by the end of the day though, as I'm either miserable from listening to Mom's worries, or we end up having another row. I know too that each day I take off, I fall behind more at school and although it niggles at me, I shrug it off. Nobody in my family seems to care about how I'm doing at school or what I'm going to do when I leave, so why should I?

As time passes, I spend more time skipping school anyway and spend the day in one of the parks in Dublin, smoking and trying to stay out of sight. I seem to be getting into a lot more trouble these days when I am in school and there are days when I just can't face it all. I was called into the principal's office for a chat the other day. Sister Columbiere (the school principal and a Carmelite nun) is a very small, quietly spoken woman with a very big presence. Capable and quite strict on the outside, she is kind and caring on the inside. Sister Columbiere sits me down, closes the door of her office (which she rarely does) and asks me if everything is okay at home, assuring me of her confidence. I say yes, that everything is fine. Then there is a long empty silence which I wish I could fill. I wish I could say that I feel like I am drowning inside and don't know what to do, that I so want to feel safe and loved and for my life to be some way normal. I want to tell her that I feel so unbelievably desolate and lonely and that nobody in my family cares about me or have my best interests at heart. I want to say so much and yet I can't say anything. What difference would it make anyway, I ask myself? What can Sister Columbiere do? What can anyone do? It's my family that is the problem and she can hardly give me a new one or wave a magic wand and make everything better, much as I would like to believe in fairy tales! I don't know much, but I do know that telling her my troubles won't change anything. I walk down the stairs from my principal's office that day with a very heavy heart and a loneliness that I will never forget.

I have started to eat more lately – comfort eating I suppose. Bars of chocolate, crisps, whatever I want really because I have also learned how to make myself sick afterwards, which takes away the guilty feeling of having gorged myself. It is becoming a bit of a habit.

I remember very little else of my earliest years. There are quite a few family photos, although I don't remember any of them being taken. Now I am glad to have them, as they are my memories. I have a black and white photograph taken when I was six. It was my first school photograph. As an adult, I have used this photo often during counselling sessions. I choose it because I saw a deep sadness in my eyes and I wanted to understand why. My expression was melancholy, not the happy, carefree face of a child. I also wanted to know why I had so few memories of my entire childhood, particularly my home life.

I had to do a lot of emotional work in counselling. How did I feel when I was six, eight and ten? How did I feel when

I was a teenager? Well, for starters, I felt different to other children. I felt anxious a lot. I was sad and very lonely inside and I felt that I was bad too; that there was something fundamentally wrong with me. I was afraid that people would find out, so I would avoid eye contact with the adults in my world, afraid of their disapproval and judgement. I was always trying to escape how I felt inside because it was so incredibly overwhelming. I remember hearing the nursery rhyme about what little girls were made of and thinking that I wasn't made of anything nice. I didn't know what was inside of me but it felt dark and ugly and I didn't know why.

My teenage years were miserable: full of anxiety, stress, fear, anger and daily drama. This only compounded and reaffirmed the feelings I had of not being good enough, of not deserving a normal happy life like my friends had. Now I was moving into adulthood, but I still felt the same way inside. I was like a house built on a very unsteady foundation: everything looked okay on the outside, but it was only a matter of time before my house fell down . . .

Chapter 2

Through the Eyes of an Adult Child

I am twenty-two years old and my life is a shambles. I don't know who I am anymore and when I look in the mirror, I see a stranger looking back at me. I am a miserable, frightened shell of a human being. So many awful things have happened in the last six years, it's hard to believe. Mom left Dad when I was eighteen and we went to America. We ran away really – how crazy is that? Dad's drinking had gone from bad to worse. Mom asked him to leave, but he naturally refused. She could have got a barring order, but knew my father wouldn't take that lightly either and was afraid of the rows and of what the neighbours would say. Mom was also afraid of how she would survive financially on her own. She hadn't worked in nearly twenty years; she had even given up driving before I was born and she obviously didn't believe that she could make it on her own. There was only Paul and me at home with Mom and she wasn't coping well anymore. We mostly lived in fear of Dad, who had become really horrible and out of control. He was so evil at times, I honestly thought he was possessed by the Devil. He didn't come home until late most nights and then the rows would begin. I remember lying in bed, waiting to hear the car pulling into the driveway and wishing that the phone would ring instead with news of another accident – a fatal one this time. I would go as far as to say that I fantasized about it regularly, imagining the funeral and all the attention and sympathy that I would get.

The weekends were even worse. I took to pleading with God to take him from us as he was making our lives so miserable. I often sat on the stairs at night, listening to the fights when he did get home, afraid that he would hurt Mom. The threats of violence had become an everyday occurrence – he even threatened to burn the house down. Mom decided that everything would be better if we went to live with Alan in Los Angeles and leaving seemed like a very good idea at the time.

Alan had done well since his move to California and he organised everything. He bought the tickets and arranged for them to be left at the Aer Lingus desk in Dublin Airport for us to collect (in case Dad found them or intercepted the postman, as he sometimes did), along with some money for the journey. It was decided that Mom and I would live with Alan, and Paul would stay with a friend of his who had gone to Los Angeles the year before and lived about an hour from where Alan was living in California.

I'll never forget the morning we left; it was March 1987 and it was a beautiful, crisp spring morning. The sky was turquoise blue and the birds were singing – carefree and oblivious – as we got into the taxi to begin our long journey. Dad was in hospital for a fictitious ear operation. He had been complaining of a buzzing noise in his ear for months, which was most likely attributable to tinnitus, but it gave my mother an idea. She went to see our family doctor and told him of our plans to leave and wanted to do it with as little fuss as possible, so together they hatched a plan for Dad to go to hospital for an overnight stay to have Dad's ear fixed. I was very fond of Doctor Healy who had treated me for the shingles, appendicitis (which turned out to be a false alarm), three lots of stitches and all the usual childhood ailments. I wasn't surprised that he helped us out and Mom said that he had wished us all the best of luck.

The house that we left that spring morning had been our seventh home since our move to Dublin, but it was also the house that we had lived in the longest, the one that felt most like home. I found out when I was around thirteen that we were renting and hadn't owned our own home since my father's business venture failed a couple of years after we moved to Dublin. I was shocked at the time and asked all my friends if their parents owned their houses, which they all did. Mom had always made excuses about why we had to move and I had always believed her. You would never have known if you walked into our house that it was rented, as it was no different to any of my friends'. Mom had the most beautiful furniture and kept a clean and tidy home. Mom's dining room was her pride and joy with a beautiful oval Georgian style mahogany table and six chairs. There was a matching display cabinet and corner cabinet filled with crystal and silverware and two silver candelabras adorned the ever polished table, which we hardly ever sat at. We lived a very middle class life on the outside and I had always naturally assumed that we were the same as everyone else. This was proof once more, as my life crumbled around me, that I was different from my friends, different from everyone I knew.

Either way, we left it all behind on that beautiful sunny morning, bringing nothing but our suitcases of clothes and a few personal belongings. I had said goodbye to all my friends, and to the village I loved, and was feeling very lonely. The reality of what we were doing hit me as the taxi driver helped us with our bags: we were leaving this house and the lives that we knew, maybe forever. It felt like we were running away – stealing away in the early morning – we hadn't even told our neighbours. It felt like a scene in a film, but then my whole life felt like one big tragic drama. My brother was delighted to be going to California; he'd spoken to his friend Tommy on the phone a few times and he was having a great time. Tommy had even managed to get Paul a job in a hotel where he worked.

When we got to the airport we went straight to the Aer Lingus desk as instructed by Alan. Thankfully, the tickets and money were there and there was nothing else to do, but leave our miserable lives behind and start over in America.

Alan took some time off work when we first arrived and showed us around Los Angeles, which was wonderful and badly needed after everything we had been through. He brought us to Disney World and Hollywood, showed us all the sights and we dined in lovely restaurants. Alan was always a very generous person and he did everything to make us feel at home, arranging for Marie (and her new boyfriend Ray) and Jack to join us when they could. Then he went back to work and expected me to do nothing other than keep Mom company all day. Alan's girlfriend Jill was also living with us, in his new suburban house in the foothills of mountains, just outside Los Angeles. It was beautiful and quiet and was idyllic at first, but I soon started to feel bored and very claustrophobic. Jill was from Cork and was only a year older than me. Mom didn't like Jill at all and neither did I. She was silly and immature and didn't seem to care about anyone but herself. Once the niceties wore off, she and my mother began to row constantly.

Six months passed and our happily-ever-after hadn't lasted very long. I couldn't go anywhere without my mother who was domineering and controlling at the best of times. If it wasn't Alan and Jill arguing, it was Mom and Jill or Mom and I, or Mom and Alan. I thought we had left all the rows behind us and I got sick of it very fast. Going out at night to a pub or club was not an option because I was only eighteen (you had to be twenty-one in California). I had been going to pubs in Dublin since I was fifteen! I had great friends at home whose company I missed and I had been used to far more freedom than this. Having friends and a social life had helped me to stay sane, but now I had nothing but my family!

My sister Marie had moved into an apartment with Ray near Huntington Beach which was two hours away from where we lived. Both of them were working full-time, so we didn't get to see them very often. We rarely saw my other brothers either, who were busy doing their own thing. I had recently received a letter from my friend Barbara who was spending the summer in London. Her older brother Patrick lived in North London and Barbara, who was studying tourism in college, had decided to spend the summer there. She'd got a job in a travel agency and was having a great time. She added at the end of her letter that I could always come to London if I didn't like California. Barbara was very genuine and I knew that she wouldn't have said that if she didn't mean it and I thought it was a great idea!

My mother was devastated and decided that she was not going to allow me to go. I begged Alan to side with me and back me up. I got him alone and told him I was really unhappy, that I had no freedom, and that I just wanted to have a bit of fun for a change.

'Anyway', I said to him in desperation, when I saw that I was losing the argument, 'you owe me.' I couldn't believe the words had come out of my mouth and I felt my face redden. There was a deafening silence that followed for what seemed like an eternity. Alan looked me straight in the eyes and I stared back defiantly. My heart was pounding and my eyes were stinging, but I held his gaze. I saw a flash of anger in Alan's eyes and thought for a moment that he might actually hit me. When he finally looked away, he lit one of his cigars and walked slowly around the driveway.

'I hope you know what you're doing,' he said eventually. 'I'll talk to Mom.'

I knew if Alan supported me, Mother would have to concede – and it worked. He even agreed to pay my fare and give me some spending money to tide me over until I got a job. Alan had his faults, but he did care for his family. I was grateful and relieved at the same time; I was also very excited. Finally, I could hope for freedom from my family and particularly from my mother. I called Barbara to tell her I was coming, but I didn't get an answer (this was during the eighties, before cell phones). I called a few times more before my flight was due to leave a week later and I still hadn't made contact. I decided to tell Mom that I had spoken to Barbara and that everything was arranged. I had her address in London and besides, I didn't care – I was sure that everything would work out fine. I felt guilty leaving Mom in the end and she was very upset, but I had to get away from her. I realised that my mother had as many issues as my father. She was controlling, manipulative, volatile, incapable of doing anything for herself and seemed to think it was everybody else's responsibility to make her happy – which was exhausting! Marie had suggested to Mom that she get a place of her own (since she didn't like Jill) but there was no question of that whatsoever. 'I didn't come all the way over to America to live by myself, I came over to be with my family,' she had insisted incredulously. Well, I had to get away from her before she swallowed me whole.

There was still no answer from Barbara when I arrived in London in late June, but I fell in love with the place from the moment I got off the plane. I took a train from Heathrow to Paddington Station, which was bustling with people of every race and colour: business men and women, students, holiday makers, back-packers and the wildest and most colourful punks I had ever seen! When I still couldn't reach Barbara on my third attempt, I decided to call my cousin Robert in Chester. My mother's sister and her husband lived in Chester for years and Robert was their only son. We visited them when I was about twelve and I enjoyed it other than Dad embarrassing us with his permanent state of drunkenness and rudeness. I got on very well with Rob (even though he was much older than me) and I decided to call him, even though I hadn't been in touch for quite a while. Thankfully, this turned out to be a great idea – he answered straight away and was delighted to hear from me. He invited me to come and stay with him until I managed to contact Barbara, so I got on a train and spent a lovely week in Chester with my cousin. Rob and I got on great and he was so good to me; he was a self-employed architect and he took the week off to spend time with me and show me the sights. Rob took me on a day trip around Wales and we had a lovely meal out; he even brought me shopping and bought me some new clothes! One night he invited friends of his, Dave, and Michelle, to dinner and he cooked us a lovely Indian curry. We drank wine and danced and I had a great time.

Barbara eventually answered the phone and she explained that she and her brother had been home in Dublin for a week due to a family bereavement. I made plans to travel back down to London the following weekend. As we were sitting in the train station, waiting for the train to London, Rob said I could always come back and live in Chester if things didn't work out elsewhere. He said he'd find me somewhere to live and I could get a job there easily enough. I thanked him for everything and was comforted by the offer. We said our goodbyes and off I went again.

London was great and I had the time of my life. Finchley was a lovely, quiet, leafy suburb where I stayed with Barbara and her brother Patrick (who had been living and working as an accountant in London for the past few years). Barbara, who loved to travel, was studying to be a travel agent in College and was working in U.S.I.T. (a student travel agency), for the summer. I got a job working in a fashion wholesaler's in Berwick Street, just off Oxford Street, and Barbara and I had an amazing summer together. We went on adventures every weekend, picnicked in Hyde Park, went to all the museums and galleries, and went to the coolest nightclubs and pubs. We even managed to see our hero, David Bowie, live in Wembley Stadium – what a brilliant night that was! We bought two cans of coke as we were leaving the stadium and they both exploded all over us. We laughed and laughed until the tears streamed down our faces. I was having so much fun for the first time in my life and I didn't want it to end. I was living in the moment, trying not to think too far ahead, but I knew Barbara would be returning to Dublin the end of September for college and I had no home there anymore and no plan for the future like all my friends had. I tried not to think about it too much, but it was always there, lurking in the back of my mind.

Claire and Donna came over from Dublin for a week's holiday in August and we all had a great time together. They had both repeated their leaving certificates' and had done well. The following Sunday after the others had left, Barbara and I went to an open air concert on Clapham Common. It was a lovely day and we had brought a rug and a picnic. As we sat in the grass in the sunshine, I felt so peaceful, as if I didn't have a care in the world. Then Barbara said, 'What are you going to do, Dee? I presume you're going to come back to Dublin, are you?'

Suddenly, it was as if the happiness had just been sucked out of the day and I felt panic rise in my throat. I knew I had to face my life again, but I didn't want to and I was scared. 'I don't know,' I said. 'Yea, I suppose I'd like to be back in Dublin. I love London but I don't think I'd like to stay here on my own. On the other hand, I have no family in Dublin anymore. I'm not sure what to do really,' I said with a heavy heart.

'Well,' Barbara said, 'you are more than welcome to come and stay with me for a while. I have already asked my parents and they're okay with it.' I was surprised, delighted and relieved at the same time and I thanked my friend and hugged her fiercely. Barbara was such a good friend to me and I felt very lucky to have her in my life.

A few weeks passed when Patrick took a call from my mother and had left a note saying to call her as soon as possible. I had a feeling of dread in my stomach as I made the call – I wasn't expecting good news. What I wasn't expecting was for her to tell me that she was returning to Ireland. She had spoken to Dad by phone a few times and had decided to go back to him. She told me that Dad said he had stopped drinking and had saved up enough money for a deposit on a house. I told her I thought she was mad.

'I can't stay here Dee; this place isn't home, at least not my home anyway. I should never have come here . . .' she trailed off sobbing.

Mom knew that I was returning to Ireland the following week as I'd told her in my last letter. She said she had already booked her flight to return the week after me and asked if I would meet with Dad when I got home and let her know what I thought. 'What's the point?' I asked. 'You've already booked your flight'. I was angry and I just knew I was going to get sucked back into their lives again, and I didn't want to have anything to do with Dad or her ridiculous decision to go back to him.

'Dee, please... For my sake?' Mom pleaded.

Why had I told her that I was going back to Dublin, I asked myself. It was too late now and I could already feel a big dark cloud gather around my head. My happy, shiny, sunny summer was over.

When I did meet my father in Dublin the following week, I hardly recognised him. His hair had gone grey, even his skin looked grey and he was so thin – he must have lost four or five stone. He drove me to a house he was renting in Clondalkin, a part of Dublin I didn't know. It was a dreary, cold house, full of old, dilapidated, mismatched furniture. My dad cried a lot and said how sorry he was, how he had changed and that he hadn't touched a drink since we left. I didn't buy any of it. I had never trusted him before, so why would I start now? I asked him where all our old furniture and belongings were? He said he had sold everything shortly after we left. He said he was sorry, that he was very angry at the time. The only things that survived were our photo albums. I called Mom later that day as promised and told her I had met him and that I still thought she was mad to go back to him. She said she had already decided. 'I have nothing left to lose and I'm not staying here,' she sobbed. 'Where else can I go and at this hour of my life? You'll be with me though Dee – won't you? I couldn't do it without you. You can't let me down now.'

I wanted to scream, 'No, you're not doing this to me – you're ruining my life!' And yet I was torn. I felt so sorry for my mother. There was a long silence before I spoke again. 'Sure Mom,' I said, with a heavy heart, and my fate for the foreseeable future was sealed. I made arrangements to meet her at the airport and live with them again. I was certain of only one thing: that it wasn't going to be any fun whatsoever. I had been enjoying my stay in Barbara's with her parents and her brother Steve. Her family were so different to mine; they were conservative and sensible, gently spoken and kind and I would much rather have stayed with them indefinitely rather than go back to living with my mother and father.

I was about to endure the most miserable time of my life so far and London soon became a distant memory. Dad had about eight thousand pounds saved. Not much of an achievement really, since he had sold all the furniture and everything else that we owned! Mom spent the money buying new furniture, saying there was no point in having a house if we had nothing to put in it. So we left Clondalkin and rented again on the north side of the city, moving three more times in the next twelve months. We eventually settled back in Skerries once again and although I was glad to be back among my friends, it just wasn't the same anymore. They were all doing different things now that we had left school and had new circles of friends.

Dad was managing to stay off the drink and he was back on the road, working in sales again. There were still rows about money every now and then and he was still incredibly mean, but other than that he was bearable. He was a strange man, really, even more so now that he was sober. He was fixated on money and never engaged in a conversation about anything else. He wasn't interested in how my day was or what I wanted to do with my life. He was only interested in his job and how many orders he had got that day and ultimately how much money he made. If Dad wasn't doing paperwork when he came home, he always seemed distracted or lost in his own thoughts. The only time my parents went out was to the occasional poker classic, something both of them enjoyed. I made an effort with him for a while, but once I realised that Dad didn't care about me – drunk or sober – I gave up.

Jack returned home soon after we moved back to Skerries too and it wasn't long before the rows broke out between him and my father. Thankfully, I had got a job working as a secretary in a freight company. Before we went to America, I had done a secretarial course and had put on my résumé that I worked as a secretary in my brother's factory, but I was still surprised when I got the job. My new boss was Peter and he was friendly and very handsome, with lovely green eyes. I liked him straight away and he brought me for lunch on the Friday of my first week. Peter told me he was thirty-one and that he was separated with a daughter Jessica, who was three. He said that he was still living in the family home for the time being, for the sake of his daughter. It sounded reasonable to me. We got on really well and within a few weeks Peter was driving me home and we were smoking joints and going for drinks after work. I loved being in his company and hated the sinking feeling I got in the pit of my stomach when he was gone.

Peter quickly became my world and everything I thought I wanted and needed. I was certainly convinced that he was the love of my life. I had been out with a couple of guys my own age, but I could never get past the friendship and the kissing. Once they tried to take things further, I'd get a sick feeling in my stomach and they would be abruptly dumped. Peter was different: he was sophisticated and unbelievably cool as far as I was concerned. He drove a very stylish BMW and he knew all the good restaurants in Dublin. His friends all had trendy apartments in the city and there was always a party on somewhere. It was all very exciting to me and was a welcome distraction from my joyless home life. When we were making out in his car for the first time, I told him that I wanted my first time to be special. Peter booked a night in a local hotel the following evening. There was a bottle of champagne cooling in an ice bucket on the table and Peter had put a red rose on the bed. It was so romantic and I felt special for the first time in my life.

A few months passed when one evening, after work, we went for our usual few drinks. Peter said he'd drop me home. I told him that my parents were out playing poker and that he could come back to the house for a while, so we picked up a bottle of wine and we left for my house. We got drunk and very stoned before we crawled into the guest room where we fell asleep, naked with no bedcovers on us. When I woke up all the lights were on and my dad was standing over the bed. I jumped up and pulled a sheet around me and pushed my father out into the landing, where he slapped me hard across the face; I slapped him back. He told me to go to bed and told Peter to get out. The next morning Dad told me to pack my bags and leave. I said I would, gladly. Finally, I was free again, though I didn't like leaving like this! Mom was crying at the front door as I walked up the driveway, but she hadn't stood up for me either, which had hurt me. I stayed with Barbara, who had come to my rescue once again. Barbara was renting a small studio apartment in Fairview where I stayed until I found a place in the city centre, sharing with a friend of a friend.

I was still working with Peter and seeing him most nights. My friends didn't like him at all, but I thought he was much more sophisticated than the guys my age. Anyway, I was in love with him! We ate out a lot and went to cool house parties, where everyone took cocaine. We had some wild nights. Peter was a regular cocaine user, which surprised me at first. Then I tried it myself and I thought I had died and gone to heaven. It took away all the fear I had inside, all the inhibitions and gave me a high that I had never experienced before. It was the perfect party drug. The come-down that I felt the next day was terrifying. I wanted cocaine again so badly that I cried. This really frightened me – I could barely function. I took it a few more times before I realised that I had to stop using it, or I wouldn't be able to.

Things started to change soon after that anyway and Peter began to make excuses about not being able to see me, especially at weekends. One night we met and he was very quiet. I knew something was up so I asked him what was bothering him. He told me he was going to go back to his wife. He said he owed it to her to give it another go for the sake of their daughter, who had been having some problems dealing with their separation. I had only met Jessica a couple of times and she was a lovely, sweet child. We went to Malahide and had fun playing in the playground there and running around the grounds of the lovely Malahide Castle. We went to the beach as well, which Jessica loved. I told Peter that I understood and wished him well, even though I was heartbroken and confused. As I climbed out of his car, the tears streamed down my face. How could this be happening? I really believed that Peter loved me and that we had something special. So why was he pulling away from the curb and driving off across the city and away from me? I felt as scared as a child left alone on a busy street corner; I was a child left alone ... I climbed under my duvet and cried for an entire week. I'll never forget the feeling of panic that I had – it was so overwhelming I couldn't catch my breath at times.

It wouldn't have been so bad if he had left it at that, but he didn't. After that first awful week, he began calling me every other day to tell me how much he missed me. I left the freight company and got a job in a fashion wholesaler in the city centre, but Peter wouldn't leave me alone. The following week he begged me to meet him. I really missed him and wanted to see him, so I gave in, and ended up meeting him regularly over the next few months. I didn't know how to say no, even when I realised that he was just using me for sex. Every time he dropped me off or left my place, I thought less and less of myself. So did my friends; they said he was just using me and couldn't understand what I was doing with him or why I was letting it continue. I didn't know either, so it was all very frustrating and my friends were getting fed up with me. I was hurting so much and I didn't know how to stop it. The following summer I went to Paris to get away from him. A friend of mine, Aisling, an art student at the time, was spending the summer there and asked me if I'd like to join her. I didn't hesitate.

I loved Paris, with its beautiful buildings and wonderful architecture. There were so many parks, trees and fountains everywhere; it was a place of incredible beauty. I got a job working in an American pizza restaurant, just off the Champs-Élysées. I worked hard and the tips were good. We had some fun too, but underneath it all I wasn't happy. I found it so hard to let Peter go and I couldn't understand why. I stayed on in Paris after Aisling went home, sharing an apartment with a mixed bunch of Europeans. One night we all got drunk and I called Peter. We talked for ages and he came over the following weekend. He stayed for a week and got fired from his job in the process. Naturally, it hadn't been a good idea at all. The first few days were fun, but then it got messy and I began to realise what a destructive person Peter really was. Not only was he hurting me, he was hurting everyone in his life – his partner, his daughter and particularly himself. I wasn't happy with him and I wasn't happy without him. What was the matter with me? I had initiated contact this time, so what was I thinking? I was just as destructive as he was. When he left Paris the following week, I fell apart. It was as if something inside me just snapped and I felt broken, utterly broken inside. Most of my teenage years were spent hoping that my life would get better, once I got away from the sinking ship that I called my family, but now I felt like I was a prisoner in my own sad, destructive, sinking ship of a life. This time, though, I didn't have anyone else to blame and what made it worse was that I didn't know how to make it any better.

A few months passed in a blur of working and sleeping until December arrived. The winter was cold, but the festive season had brought warmth to the city again. The rows of light-filled trees on the Champs-Élysées were particularly bright and beautiful. Christmas-time in Paris was magical and I was doing my best to be cheerful, but once again I felt like I was just going through the motions. I was miserable and didn't know what to do for Christmas, never mind what I was going to do with my life. I knew I didn't want to stay in Paris forever.

The lack of taxis after work was a nuisance at the best of times, particularly at the weekends, but especially during the run up to Christmas. I stood queuing at the taxi-rank on the Champs-Élysées in the early hours of a Sunday morning, after a very busy night's work. I was tired and cold and there were lots of people waiting at the rank, so after nearly an hour I decided to walk home. I lived less than ten minutes away, in the fifth *arrondissement* (or district), but as I walked down the long boulevard that would bring me to my apartment I began to feel frightened. Before I turned my head to look behind me, I knew I was in danger and I felt a chill run right

45

through me. The moment I looked around, this dark hooded figure began to run towards me. I ran too, although it felt like I was moving in slow motion. The street was empty and there weren't even any doors that I could knock on. He came up like a shadow behind me, threw me against a wall and pulled my bag from my shoulder. He was tall and was wearing a tracksuit, with the hood pulled over his head. All I could see were the whites of his eyes, as his skin was as dark as his clothes in the night sky. I thought he was going to kill me. He had something else in his hand, in front of my face, and the next moment my eyes and face were burning; the heat and the pain were intense.

I don't know how much time had passed, but the next thing I remember is hearing a distant scream. It got louder and louder until I realised that it was me, screaming repeatedly. I didn't even recognise my own voice. My face, head and hands felt like they were on fire and I was completely blind. Soon after a taxi driver stopped and brought me home. He wanted to drive me but I wouldn't get into his car; I couldn't even see him. I gave him my address and he very kindly walked me to my apartment and waited for someone to answer. One of my flatmates, Jonathan, a really nice guy from London, brought me in and called a doctor and the police straight away. The doctor explained that my mugger had sprayed industrial mace on my face and in my eyes; this was why my head was burning too as I had put my hands to my head without realising. I couldn't see for two days and had to have bandages around my eyes, face and hands. The police said there was nothing they could do, that it was just another random mugging, probably for drug money, and advised me never to walk home alone again.

Everyone was very kind to me and I received lots of flowers and chocolates. The company that I worked for changed their policy and began booking taxis for staff at the end of the night, so some good came out of it. Just as I was recovering and was back in work, my face began to swell up and I felt very unwell. I went to the company doctor and he referred me to a dermatologist. I called Dr Healy back in Skerries the next morning when I saw that I had blood in my urine. He told me that I probably had a nasty kidney infection and advised me to get home to Dublin, if I could, and he would start treatment immediately. He said that with my family history, especially my brother Jack who had kidney trouble as a teenager, it would be best if I came home until I was better. I managed to get an emergency passport (as mine had been stolen with my handbag) and got a flight home to Dublin just two days before Christmas. My fate had been decided for me once more. I spent the next three weeks in bed in my parents' house, with Doctor Healy calling every evening. I even slept through my twenty-first birthday in January.

Once I began to feel better, I decided not to return to Paris, not even to collect my belongings or clothes. I rang my closest flatmate, Sylvie, and told her she could do what she liked with my stuff – she wasn't very impressed with me.

My good and faithful friends arranged a night out to celebrate my birthday as soon as I was feeling better again. It was nearing the end of January and we all met up in a city centre pub. It was great to see them again and they were all doing different things – some still in college and others working. I caught up on all the news over a lovely meal: who was going out with who, who had finished up with who and any other gossip that I'd missed. I told them about

Peter coming over to Paris, and about the mugging and the subsequent kidney infection. I could see the frustration and bewilderment in their faces.

'Why did you let that reptile back into your life?' Donna said. 'I thought you went to Paris to get away from him. When are you going to learn Dee? He's just a user and a selfish bastard.' My eyes filled with tears – she was right of course. 'I'm sorry,' she said, 'it's just you deserve so much better, doesn't she everyone?' Everyone else agreed and I tried to smile. I was just as frustrated as they were. What was wrong with me? Why couldn't I be more like Donna – she didn't take shit from anyone!

I started to look for an apartment to rent in Dublin. I also began to look for a job. I had saved most of my tips from my waitressing job in Paris so I had enough money to get by for a while anyway. I also met with Peter for the first time since returning from France, but this time it was different – it was on my terms. I felt that I needed to get closure with him and there were things that I needed to say to him. I knew that it was finally over between us and yet I was surprised to find when I met him that I felt nothing at all. It was a strange experience to see him without the rose-tinted glasses; he looked old and tired and grey. He also seemed deeply unhappy. I told Peter that all he did was hurt the people around him and that he'd used my feelings for him to hurt me and use me in the past, but that I had finally realised this and I wasn't going to let it happen again. I wished him well as I got out of his car and I felt a huge amount of relief as I said goodbye. I was free again and hoped, rather than believed, that everything would improve for me from this point on.

One of the jobs I applied for was in another fashion wholesaler and there was even a small company car on offer. I didn't think I had a chance of getting it, but I did! I couldn't believe my luck. I did say I had a full license when I only had a provisional one. Dad had been driving without a license all his life and he had never been caught, so I didn't give it much thought. I applied to do the test straight away and hoped I wouldn't get caught in the meantime. I also found a nice apartment, sharing with another girl, just around the corner from Merrion Square. Maybe this would be the start of a new life; maybe I could finally be happy.

I started to go out again with my old friends, although it was different now, as most of them were in relationships and were socialising in different circles. They had new friends and lots going on in their lives – normal stuff really – but I felt that life was moving forward and leaving me behind. Everything was changing, which I didn't like; it was all very frightening to me. I didn't realise how dependent I was on my friends being there for me. I felt awkward and self-conscious going out with Donna and Claire and their boyfriends and their gang of friends; or Suzanne and her boyfriend and his friends. Aisling had lots of new friends and had become so confident – I hardly recognised her. I didn't feel like I belonged anywhere anymore, which made me feel isolated and very lonely. When Peter came into my life, I abandoned my friends. I knew that my behaviour had hurt them – I had let them down many times and they had learned not to depend on me anymore. I never felt that I was in control of anything when I was involved with Peter and I had never intended to hurt anyone, but I had and it bothered me a lot.

It was also entirely my fault, as far as I could see, and I began to despise myself even more.

The job was turning out to be a bit of a disaster too. My boss was as tough as nails and there was a lot of pressure to sell, sell, sell. The problem was that orders were always wrong, or the items were faulty and it seemed to me that they had burned their bridges wherever I went looking. Customers were always complaining or had left for another supplier. I got on well with one of the other reps, Yvonne, who was laid back and didn't let the pressure bother her, but I didn't like it at all and I dreaded the sales meetings. We started to go out together at night or after work. Yvonne was single too and was actively looking for a relationship. I definitely wasn't looking for a relationship but that didn't stop me from bringing a guy home for the night because I was lonely; often someone I had just met. I usually cried afterwards and felt worthless and ashamed, but then I'd do it again a few weeks later.

One night, during the week, I went for a walk as I often did with my headphones on. I was coming down Grafton Street when I met Claire's boyfriend James and his friend David. They were both on a day off and had been betting on the horses earlier in the day and had won. Naturally, they went straight to the pub and were now on an official 'pub crawl'. I joined them for a drink and we ended up in a wine bar some hours later. At one point, I walked home to get some more money (as they had been buying drinks all night and were now broke) and very stupidly decided to drive back to meet them. Why didn't I just go home that night and stay home!

The boys were very drunk at this stage as they had been drinking most of the day as well. When we decided to leave, James picked up a rucksack that he thought was David's.

David was a stagehand and nearly always had one with him, except that on this occasion he had left it at home earlier that day. When we got into the car, James threw the rucksack into David's lap and gave out to him for forgetting it. David opened up the bag and had a rummage in it before he realised that the bag wasn't his. 'You gobshite, Jamie,' he said. 'This isn't my bag. I left mine at home earlier.' Just then there was a knock on the window; it was one of the security men from the wine bar. James explained his mistake and said he was just about to return the bag but the security man wouldn't listen and insisted on calling the police. I couldn't believe it, but thought that if I stayed calm and just explained what happened, everything would be okay. I spoke to one of the police officers when they arrived, explaining to him how James had mistaken the bag for David's. He wasn't convinced. 'Why,' I asked, 'would anyone rob a student's rucksack?' He still wasn't listening and said that the young man who owned the bag was adamant that we had taken it on purpose and wanted to press charges.

We were standing beside my company car, which was very noticeable as it completely covered with company logos. 'Is that your car Miss?' the guard asked. I replied that it was. 'Were you thinking of driving it home?' he asked. 'No, of course I wasn't,' I replied. 'Well, you'd better give me the keys so,' he said.

We were arrested, brought down to the police station and charged with larceny. I didn't even know what larceny meant at the time!

They even put me in a cell on my own and left me there until early the next morning. I couldn't believe it – I thought I was going to wake up any minute from what was turning into a horrible nightmare. Unfortunately, the arresting officer knew my new boss as the station was close to where I worked. I was called into my boss's office the next day and fired on the spot. She said that I was a bad reflection on the image of the company. 'That nice guard from Pearse Street station called me this morning and told me everything,' she said. 'He was so obliging; he even drove the car here this morning. Well, you won't be driving it again,' she said smugly. I hadn't a leg to stand on so I turned on my heels and walked home. I had been with the company for less than four months and consoled myself with the knowledge that it wasn't a good job to lose and I had hated every moment working there.

We had to appear in court the following morning; the whole thing was a blur to me. In the end, the case was dropped, but to this day, I will never understand how it all happened. Unfortunately, the events of that night would change my life and set me on a much more perilous path . . .

Not to be deterred, I got a job in a nightclub a couple of days later, working from Thursday night through to Sunday night. I didn't like it much, but it paid the rent and kept me out of the pub. A few months later, I got a second job, as I needed the extra money as I really wanted to buy a car. It was another waitressing job in a popular Italian restaurant off Grafton Street. I worked the lunchtime shift, which I enjoyed; the other waitresses were really nice and the atmosphere was warm and friendly.

I did not tell my family what had happened with the sales job, other than to say that it didn't work out. Mom and Dad, at any rate, had a lot on their minds at the time, as they had recently decided to move back to the southeast of the country with my two brothers. Paul had recently returned home from the States and was going to move down with them too. Mom was not so pleased, even though it was her idea to move, but renting was getting too expensive in Dublin and they just couldn't afford it anymore. Dad had wanted to go to back to Kilkenny, but Mom said no – she couldn't face that. They had been successful in Kilkenny and had plenty of money then. She didn't want to go back there with nothing. Dad was still working as a sales rep and travelled all over the country so it didn't really matter to him where they were based.

I called out to see them the day before they left. There were the all-too-familiar boxes, packed and stacked up everywhere. I was glad not to be going with them this time, but as I gave Mom a hug she cried and said she wished they didn't have to go. I felt so sorry for her again. She loved the sea and going for walks out alone the coast road. I had often gone with her and loved it too. I knew she would miss it. Mom hadn't renewed any of the friendships she had when she returned from America. I was the only goodbye Mom had to make, other than Aunty Katie, who Mom said was being very cool with her on the phone when she called to say her goodbyes. Mom looked tired and weary from it all; there was something resigned about her, as if she really had given up. I wished I could have waved a magic wand and given her the home and the stability she so wanted. I had no wand and happy endings didn't seem to feature in my life either. It would be strange for me too, not having my family based in Dublin anymore; I couldn't imagine them living somewhere else in Ireland.

October came and with it a phone call from my cousin, Ellie, who had never contacted me directly before. She said that she and Sarah wanted to talk to me about something and asked if I would meet them in Kildare the following Sunday. I hadn't seen my cousins in a few years, so I was surprised and more than a bit puzzled with her request, but arranged to meet them in the pub they suggested at two o'clock the following Sunday. What did they want to talk to me about? Well, I would soon find out. She sounded so serious on the phone...

Ellie and Sarah were sitting at a table looking a little nervous when I joined them. I'd caught the one o'clock train down so I'd have plenty of time. They looked older and more sophisticated since the last time we had met and their welcome could hardly be described as warm. I wondered if I had done something to offend them. It had been a late finish at the club the night before and I was tired. Now I was tired and uncomfortable. As soon as we had got past the pleasantries, Ellie asked me a question that floored me completely:

'Do you remember the time I asked you – we would've been around six or seven – if your daddy tickled you the way he tickled me?'

'What?' I asked incredulously. What sort of a question was that? What was she talking about? 'No,' I said after a minute, 'I don't remember any such conversation.'

'Are you sure Deirdre?' Sarah asked. 'Try to think back.'

'I think I'd remember something like that' I answered, a little testily.

Ellie insisted that she had asked me this question a few times when we were children and that I had run off and ignored her. I explained to them that my memory was very bad and that I remembered little of my early childhood. Still, they seemed suspicious and as they asked more questions, I began to feel that I was being interrogated. Eventually they seemed to believe me, and then went on tell me of the many different occasions when my dad had sexually assaulted them, particularly my cousin Sarah. I was shocked and stunned and didn't know what to say. I did remember Dad was obsessive about buying sweets and ice cream for our cousins, and sometimes brought Sarah to the shop as his helper, but that was all I could remember.

My mind began filling up with questions that I had no answers to. What was going on? Why were my cousins behaving as if it was my fault, and why was I feeling guilty? I thanked Ellie and Sarah for telling me, as I didn't know what else to do. Sarah said she had already made a statement to the police who would be in contact with my father to get a statement from him. She added that this was the main reason for meeting me – to tell me about making the statement to the police and to find out if I already knew something. Sarah then said that it was up to me if I wanted to let the rest of my family know, but that either way the police would be calling to my father at some point in the not-to-distant future. My head began to spin and I suddenly felt very nauseous. I said my goodbyes and left. There were no hugs or kisses, just silence, as I walked out the door. I was reeling in the shock of it all and my legs could hardly carry me.

I sat on a bench in the train station and lit a cigarette. The next moment, the strangest thing happened: I got a flashback – a memory that came back to me out of the blue. It was as clear as a movie screen and it was playing as large as life in my head. I was sitting in the back of Dad's car with my friend Sophie and my brother. Sophie's sister Ann was sitting in the front with Dad. It was a Saturday morning and we were going swimming. I must have been about seven, as was Sophie. I could clearly see Dad lean across the seat and rub Ann's leg up and down. Next he put his hand up her skirt and he was moving it around. It went on for what seemed like ages and I remember my face burning hot as I looked out the window because I didn't know what else to do. I remember feeling dirty inside and not knowing why.

The arrival of the train brought me back to reality and I suddenly felt dizzy and sick. As I stood, smoking out the window of the train, I try to make sense of what had just happened. What Ellie and Sarah had told me must have triggered this other memory. I was feeling devastated for all of them, but with Ann I felt somehow responsible, maybe because I was there, or maybe because of my friendship with Sophie. Ann was a quiet, gentle, shy girl who was polite, well-mannered and very kind. She would have been only eight or nine then. How could my father have done such a thing? Who else had he done this to, I wondered? I noticed that my hands were shaking and my knees were beginning to buckle under me, so I made my way to a carriage and sat down. Somehow, everything started to make sense and fall into place as I began to remember more. I tried desperately to stop the doors of my mind from opening up and revealing the truth of my past, but I couldn't. I was remembering my father's voice now and how it would change sometimes, become low and gravelly and how that would make me feel sick in my tummy. Panic swelled up from my gut and gripped my neck like a noose... I see myself being bounced up and down on his lap and it makes me shiver. Stop.... Stop.... was all I could remember. I wanted it to stop. I always wanted it to stop. I can hardly breathe and I try to think of something happy. My days at the stables and Bobby soon fill my mind and before I know it I am back in the city and heading back to the apartment where I lived, a place that did not feel remotely like home. I really wished I was going home to a warm fire and someone to talk to, someone to hug me and tell me everything would be okay.

Ciara was my flatmate and she worked one week on and one week off. She went home to Cavan the weeks she was off so she was hardly ever there. The apartment was empty and cold as it so often was and I felt so unhappy I wanted to hurt myself again. I pounded my fists off the wall – and then my head – until I had a really bad headache. I smoked, what must have been my twentieth cigarette, before going to bed, where I tossed and turned for the night.

I didn't want to tell my mother over the phone about meeting my cousins, so I decided to wait until I went down to Tipperary for Christmas; I could only hope that the police wouldn't get there first. I had promised Mom I'd come down for a week or two if I could. God, how was I going to tell my mom and how would I face *him*. I thought my life could not possibly get any worse – I was meant to have my whole life ahead of me and yet I felt so tired of it all. Life just seemed so miserable and bleak; good things didn't happen to me and there never was the happy endings that I so loved to watch on television. I was barely able to survive financially even though I worked day and night as a waitress. I didn't realise how ashamed I was about my job until some of my old school friends came into the restaurant for lunch. They had all gone to college and were doing well for themselves and I cringed as the old feelings of inferiority haunted me once again.

There was a party on in Skerries the following week-end and Donna had invited me over for the night. Donna's boyfriend Greg and Claire's boyfriend James were part of a large group of friends and one of them, Patrick, who lived in London, was home for a few weeks and was throwing a party. I decided to go as I thought it might cheer me up and it would be nice to see my friends. Patrick, who was painfully thin and pale, was also funny and self-deprecating, and a bit off-the-wall too. His father was a builder and his mother had died when he was very young (just like Peter, funnily enough). I ended up in bed with him at the end of the night, but before anything happened Patrick told me he was HIV positive. He explained that he was an ex-heroin addict and was on a methadone programme in a London clinic. I didn't care and I wanted to have sex with him anyway. Thankfully, Patrick was not just a funny guy, he was a decent human being and he refused. We did continue a relationship of sorts for a while and we did have sex too, after Patrick got advice about safe sex from his clinic. Patrick was another damaged person, although he was very sweet. I began to see just how damaged he was after a while, but he would never do anything to hurt me and he was kind and caring.

I came to my senses as I sat in one of Dublin's A&E departments a couple of weeks later, at about five o'clock in the morning. Patrick was getting withdrawals as he had not returned to London and had run out of his methadone. He was shivering, sweating and shaking and was getting contrary with the nurses. One of the nurses called me into a separate cubicle and asked me to sit down. She was a very pleasant middle-aged woman and I had no idea what she was going to say next, but I've never forgotten it. She asked me the usual questions at first: my name, my age and where I lived. I told her. She asked my relationship with Patrick; how long were we together and did I know about his HIV diagnosis? I said yes. She then looked at me with the concerned face of a mother and said, 'I hope you don't think I'm sticking my nose in, I'm just very concerned about you. *Do you know what you're doing Deirdre*?' she asked. I looked at her blankly, not knowing what to say. She had said the words softly, but with such incredulity and it had left me a little shocked. 'Look, you seem like a lovely girl,' she continued, 'and you have your *whole life* in front of you. I have a daughter your age and, well, I'd hate to think....it's just......please, don't throw your life away like this.' I told her that Patrick was very kind and she said, 'I'm sure he is, but do you know the risks involved, because you are taking a huge risk? Don't you want to have children one day? Do you really want to risk your life for him?' I started to cry, more so because she cared than because of anything she said.

Over the next few days, the nurse's words rolled around inside my head and wouldn't let up. I decided that she was right and I ended it with Patrick, who went back to London shortly afterwards. The way I chose to deal with it at the time was not to deal with it, not process it at all. I was going around on auto-pilot and just buried the whole business. That's the only way I can describe it and I didn't do it intentionally, but it's like Patrick never happened, and I just continued on, working in the restaurant by day and the club by night. It shocked me to the core in later years, when I'd recall how I had such little regard for my life at the time. It was like playing a game of Russian roulette with my life and the worst part was that I didn't seem to care about myself at all. The fact that the nurse cared had made a difference. She may well have saved my life that morning and I'm grateful to her, whoever she was.

Christmas was coming and the nightclub that I worked for were having their annual festive night out. As the club was open Thursday to Sunday, Wednesday was to be our night out and as the night drew closer I began to look forward to it. Complimentary tickets to a gig at the Olympia Theatre and a few drinks afterwards at a late night venue were on offer and it was staff only, so I didn't have to worry about bringing someone. Besides Gary, who was one of the barmen at the club, was very cute! He had walked me home a couple of times after work as he said he lived nearby. We'd even had an occasional snog. Little did I know that this particular night out was going to change my life.

Wednesday came and I had a long bath after my lunch-time shift at the restaurant. I was in better form than I had been in a while and was determined to make the best of it. I decided to wear a shimmery red halter-neck top and a pair of black velvet hot pants that I had just bought, with black knee-high boots and black tights. It was probably the most daring thing I had ever worn! There wasn't a pick on me with all the work I was doing and I told myself I looked great as I threw on my coat and left my apartment.

The band in the Olympia was great and the atmosphere was really good. I was enjoying myself for the first time in ages. When we were all leaving to go to another pub, Gary side-lined me and said he had to meet a friend of his in another pub nearby and asked me to come with him. I said no at first, but he persisted, saying we'd just have one drink and meet up with the others again in Leeson Street. I reluctantly agreed and found myself in a not so salubrious bar full of men and I quickly became very uncomfortable. Gary's friend gave me the creeps. He was a biker type in his mid-thirties with shoulder-length black hair and very dark eyes. Gary went to the bar and I remember him handing me a shot and a pint. I said I didn't want the shot, but he said 'just one, for Christmas.' I noticed that both of them seemed to be watching me as I drank it, encouraging me to knock it back. They were already half way through their pints and were encouraging me to drink mine. There was another drink already on the table. Something didn't feel right, but I didn't know what it was. I said to Gary that we'd better get going, but he replied that we had plenty of time. I wish I'd left then and gone home, or gone back to the party, but I didn't.

I don't remember much more after that. I started to feel dizzy and my arms and legs began to feel very heavy. I became really sluggish and felt like I was looking at the world through a keyhole. I knew I wasn't drunk, as I had only had a couple of drinks earlier. After that, everything happened so fast. Gary offered to bring me out for some fresh air and I vaguely remember leaving the pub with Gary on one side of me and his friend on the other. I knew then that something was very wrong; I was practically being carried down the street and at this point I couldn't even open my mouth to ask for help. I remember being in a taxi sandwiched between Gary and his mate. Then I completely blanked out and there's nothing but darkness – sickening, awful darkness.

I came around slowly and realised that I was lying on a floor. There was someone kneeling behind my head, holding my wrists really tightly. I looked up and saw that the person holding me down was Gary. There was something stuffed in my mouth. Then I noticed that Gary's friend was straddling me. I had no awareness of what he was doing at the time; it was as if my body was disconnected from my mind. I couldn't feel anything other than the pain in my wrists. When I looked at his face I thought, *he is going to kill me.* His face was contorted with what could only be described as pure hatred as he spat out an endless stream of profanities. I was asking for it 'dressed like that', I was nothing but a cock tease ... that I deserved all I was getting. I was a worthless whore and a slut. I was nothing ... On and on it went. Was he going to choke me or slit my throat, I wondered to myself. He, and I've never been able to remember his name (I can only presume it was false anyway) was obviously raping me, but I felt nothing. I looked around to see where I was and was both shocked and relieved to see that this was my bedroom floor. I saw my clothes strewn around and I wondered how long I had been there.

The next thing that I see is a very shiny, sharp-looking knife in front of my face. This is it I thought – terrified – as I felt the sharp blade pushing into the side of my neck. I closed my eyes, certain that he was going to slit my throat. I hoped it wouldn't hurt too much and wondered what the hot blood would feel like, running down my neck and chest.

'I'm going to kill you,' he said. 'Do you understand? If you open your mouth about this to anyone, yeah, I'll be watching you. Every move you make – I'll be watching. I'll slit your throat when you're in bed – you won't even wake up – you'll never wake up again. Is that clear?' I barely nod because of the knife pressing into my throat. He took what had been stuffed in my mouth out, threw it on the floor and put the knife to my lips. 'Not – a – word – bitch. I know where you live.'

With that, they both left, talking about deals and drugs. Gary even said goodbye, as if nothing had happened. As I locked and bolted the door I noticed the first light of dawn appearing in the dark sky. *So it was nearly morning* I thought. I knocked on Ciara's door and there was no answer. I went into her room before remembering that she had gone home to Cavan for the week, as she usually did. I had told Gary this earlier in the night too. He asked and I just thought he was making small talk. . . . Oh, what a fool I was! Gary had sold me like a piece of meat, and I had made it so easy for him.

I started to shake uncontrollably. I went into the bathroom and ran a bath. Going back to my room I picked up my torn clothes from the floor – even my necklace was broken and lying on the carpet. How could I not remember any of this? I took the clothes, including the boots and threw them in the bin. Then I climbed into the scalding hot bath and started to scrub myself all over. My legs and thighs were already bruised. My neck was bruised. My wrists had bruises all the way around; they were the imprints of Gary's hands and that really freaked me out. It felt like he was still holding me and although I kept scrubbing until my skin was red and sore, I couldn't wash him off. Having a bath didn't make me feel any cleaner – I still felt dirty. I would probably never feel clean again. And I felt more afraid than I had ever been in my life.

I put my pyjamas on and sat, curled up in an armchair in the sitting room for hours, with a blanket wrapped around me, listening to one of my favourite albums on the stereo, over and over again. I rocked myself to and fro constantly, something I had never done before. The phone rang a few times, but I didn't answer it. I knew I was supposed to be in work at the bistro, but I could only get up to press the replay button on the stereo. Eventually, I heard the intercom bell ring and I became paralyzed with fear. I didn't move. My heart was beating so loudly I could hear it. The bell rang again. I got up and pressed down the speaker button, without saying anything. 'Dee. . . Dee, it's Sharon. Are you there?' Sharon was a friend of mine from the restaurant. I remembered that I was supposed to meet her at some stage. I buzzed her in and before I knew it, my knees had buckled under me and I was crying on the floor with relief.

Sharon made me some hot sweet tea and was very kind. I remember very little else; I presume that I must have been in shock. I know that I didn't want to be on my own and I pleaded with Sharon to stay with me, which she did. She wanted me to go to the Rape Crisis Centre, but I became hysterical at the thought of leaving the apartment. She made me promise to go with her the next morning and we did. Sharon called a taxi to take us there and back. I was told that I had probably been given rohypnol, which, the counsellor explained, was a 'date rape' drug. I'd never heard of rohypnol or 'date rape', but the counsellor was very kind and sympathetic and advised me to go to a doctor or hospital straight away. I was also encouraged to contact the police and make a statement about what had happened. I didn't take any of the advice given. I didn't go to the doctor, the hospital or the police – they were simply not options for me at that time. I was completely and utterly paralyzed by fear. I just wanted to stay alive now and that meant only one thing to me – I had to vanish. *It's not safe being me,* I kept thinking to myself.

I felt even worse as I left the centre – it had become so much more real to me by this time. I felt like a statistic, a victim. Of course I *was* a victim and I didn't feel safe anymore. I had learned that much from the counsellor, which was more important than I realised at the time, because at least

I didn't blame myself completely. Thankfully, Sharon stayed with me again that night and though she pressed me to go to a doctor, she knew to leave it alone by my reaction. I called home and Mom answered. I couldn't speak for ages; I just cried and cried.

'What has happened?' she kept asking, 'what's wrong, Dee?' How could I possibly tell her? Eventually I asked if I could come home for a while, saying that I really needed to get out of Dublin. Mom said she would send my brother up for me the next day if I wanted. I told her that would be great and cried so much with relief that I couldn't say goodbye. I slept soundly for a few hours with Sharon beside me. As soon as I woke, I got up and started to pack my things and put them together in the hall. I made some coffee and woke Sharon, as I knew she had to go to work.

I hugged her and thanked her. She cried and asked me to keep in touch. As she was leaving, she turned to me. 'Take care of yourself Dee,' she said. I only wished that I knew how; I couldn't even trust myself anymore. I blamed myself in so many ways for what had happened: my poor judgment, my big mouth, my trusting nature, my stupidity and my naivety! Even what I chose to wear had made it my fault.

When my brother arrived later that morning in a white Hi ace van he hugged me, something he rarely did. He took one look at me and I knew he wouldn't ask any questions, because I knew he didn't want to know the answers. Not because he didn't care – I knew he did – but because it was easier to say nothing. So there was mostly silence on the way down to Tipperary, occasionally interrupted by a little small talk, which suited me fine. We both smoked, so nothing was said as I smoked one cigarette after another. When we arrived to a strange house that was to be home for a while, Mom was there to greet me. She hugged me very tightly and I cried again.

The house was quite nice. It was a big four-bedroom house built on a hill, overlooking the town. Home to me was being around my mom – I needed her now and being under her roof and away from Dublin made me feel safe for the moment. Christmas came and went without much fuss. Any day that was dry, Mom and I went for a long walk. She never asked me about Dublin and what had happened.

Nightmares became a regular occurrence for me and I woke up most mornings drenched in sweat. Sometimes I wondered if I might be HIV positive, and then I would push that thought away into the closet along with all my other skeletons. One morning I woke to the sound of unfamiliar voices at the front door. I got up and looked out the window. There was a squad car outside. I immediately thought about Ellie and Sarah and was filled with dread. I had completely forgotten and hadn't said anything to Mom. Maybe it was something else; *please let it be something else.* I dressed quickly and ran down to Mom in the kitchen, who looked bewildered. The voices were now coming from the living room and I could hear Dad's voice among them.

'They wanted to speak to your dad,' she said. 'There were two of them. What has he done now?' she asked, and before I could answer, she said, 'Oh, never mind that for now ... Happy birthday Dee! I'm sorry it's not much,' she said with a worried smile, as she handed me a card with a gift-token for the local book shop. I hadn't remembered that it was my birthday – something I had never forgotten before! I thanked Mom and gave her a hug. Then I remembered the squad car and I wasn't sure what to do. I decided to wait and see what Dad was going to say.

I went back to my bedroom and sat in front of the mirror. I hardly recognised the person looking back at me. *Twenty-two years old and look at the state of you* I said to myself. My eyes looked vacant to me, like a stranger's. I looked tired, pale and gaunt with dark circles around my eyes. I hardly ate anything and I only went out when I had to. I was afraid to go anywhere alone. I was afraid of crowds, especially of anyone coming up behind me – this gave me such a fright, that my knees would buckle underneath me every time. I didn't even know what day it was anymore and I was back living at home, which was depressing and miserable, with no desire to do anything or to be anywhere else. I didn't know who I was anymore; I was a stranger to myself. I didn't trust myself and I felt like a complete failure. So many bad things had happened to me in the last year, and as I looked in the mirror I really believed that I must have deserved it all. Now there was a police car outside our front door and a can of the most horrible worms was about to be well and truly opened; that sinking feeling was back ... *slugs and snails and puppy dog tails*, was ringing in my ears again.

Winter

I walk parallel to the river,
Its dark waters twisting and swirling, as it passes me.
For a moment I am totally drawn; transfixed,
as her soft voice whispers to me,
calling me into her cool flowing mass.

My body aches, longing to feel the cool water
surround and seduce me –
pulling me into her mysterious depths.
A fleeting reflection breaks my trance.
I look up and see a skylark:
light and free,
soaring and diving through the sky.
I turn and walk away,
weary of my heavy feet on the ground.

(River Suir, 1993)

Chapter 3

Growing Up for Real

My name is Deirdre and I am forty-five years old. Most people call me Dee. I am lucky to have a few good friends and I value their friendship very much. My husband Jimmy is my best friend. I am happy to report that not only have I have survived my past, but I am very well and also, thankfully, very happy. When I was twenty-two, I honestly didn't think I would live to be twenty-three, nor did I care particularly. Now I am very happily married to a man whom I love dearly and who loves me more than I could have ever have imagined. We have three amazing children and we have a wonderful home that is our own. We are a happy family and I value this so much. I have worked very hard for the love and the harmony that I now have in my life. Our children have structure and routine in their lives, and above all, they have loving caring parents that they can depend on. I am proud of this, as is my husband Jimmy. I love my life, I love my family and I love myself. I wouldn't change a thing now; not even the choices that I made in my past.

I know who I am now, too, which is a great relief, as I'm not made of slugs and snails and puppy-dog tails! I'm strong, courageous, determined, loving and forgiving. I'm also stubborn, head-strong, intolerant and inflexible at times. I'm human and I'm flawed and that's okay – I'd be unbearable if I was perfect anyway! Finding my truth and what is real in this challenging world of ours is very important to me. I am constantly learning and growing and I have learned how to process my feelings and to communicate my feelings and thoughts to others when I need to. It's not all a bed of roses either; my life has had its ups and downs and I have been challenged at times, both financially and in my relationships. Jimmy and I have struggled to support ourselves and our family at times. There are also times when we're all rowing and bickering, but that's part of life and I wouldn't change it for anything.

No matter how complex or challenging my life can be, I believe that I have been given the tools and the talents to overcome the difficult times and to learn from them. I also believe that we can change our current reality; we do not have to be defined by our past experiences. I could have been a prostitute, an alcoholic or a drug addict. I could have chosen to end my life. Thankfully, I didn't make any of these choices and I am aware of how lucky I am to be alive, given some of the choices that I did make. I am not a victim of my life anymore. It wasn't an easy journey for me and change didn't happen overnight. I travelled down some more familiar paths and allowed myself to hurt some more before I really hit rock bottom and looked for help. I consider myself lucky: so many people let fear get in the way and they spend their lives running from their past and their pain. I very nearly did too. First, the story of my family continued. . .

The day the police called to the house, my dad admitted that he had sexually assaulted my cousin Sarah. The DPP decided to prosecute, given that my father admitted the charges, though Dad was furious for weeks afterwards, claiming that he had been caught off guard. He said that his version of things had been 'misunderstood', that he explained to the guard that he had dropped ice cream on Sarah's lap by accident and that things had gotten out of hand! The case took a year to come before the local circuit court and none of our family attended the court, other than Dad obviously. Aunty Katie, Uncle Des and cousin Ellie were there to support Sarah, but we did not hear from any of them. It was obviously something Sarah needed to do and we were all supportive of her. Aunty Katie phoned Mom when it was all over and explained that Sarah did not wish to have any further contact with any of our family, ever again. She added that Sarah had also insisted that Katie, Des and Ellie were to have no further contact with of our family either – no phone calls, no letters, nothing. Poor Mom was devastated; Katie was the only family she had and they had always been close. It felt like we were all being blamed for what Dad had done.

In the end, although Dad was found guilty of sexually assaulting my cousin, he received only a three year suspended sentence and didn't have to spend a single night in jail! He laughed at the sentence – laughed – saying that even the judge mustn't have thought it was a serious crime. I remember feeling sick to my stomach when I heard the verdict. Was there no justice in the world? I was so disappointed, both for Sarah and for all victims of sexual abuse. It had certainly given my father the wrong message.

Sarah maintained her anonymity, as was her right, but requested that my father be named and his details be made available to the media. So he was named in the local and all the national newspapers, along with his age, address, marital status and *'he lived at this address with his wife and three adult children.'* There could be no confusion about who he was and therefore, who we were either. Nobody protected us. I found this very difficult to cope with at the time, as did my mother, and it was even harder on Jack and Paul. Did Sarah not realise how much she was hurting us by doing this? Each one of us felt embarrassed and ashamed and found it all very overwhelming. Dad didn't care: he was the only one who didn't seem to be affected by any of this. Why didn't he hang his head in shame? Why were his sons hanging their heads instead? I was angry with Sarah and believed that she was acting on a desire to hurt Dad, but was only hurting us in the process. Looking back, I realise that Sarah did what she felt she needed to at the time and she showed an enormous amount of courage in the process. Why wouldn't she want to hurt and humiliate Dad, when he had hurt her so much? Why would she not want justice for what he had done? She had every right to do what she did. What right had I to be angry with her? I was really angry with Dad, but I didn't realise that until quite some time later.

Unfortunately, neither Sarah nor Ellie have ever spoken to me since I met them that Sunday afternoon in Kildare. I know Sarah, in particular, was very hurt and was just trying to heal her own pain. I think of them often and, thankfully, I have let go of the hurt and anger that I felt at the time of Dad's trial. I hope that they are happy and have peace in their lives. Speaking the truth about abuse in families can be painful and can tear families apart, but it is a necessary process. It gives everyone the opportunity to heal. When Ellie and Sarah spoke to me about what happened to them, I started to remember my own painful memories, which enabled me to begin to heal (when I was ready) from all that had happened to me. Had they been silent, I may never have remembered what I witnessed and what happened to me, and I may have spent my life wondering what was wrong with me.

I was working in the sales office of a small manufacturing company when my father's final court hearing took place and was publicised in all the papers. It was a nightmare that had now become a very public reality. By the end of the week, I knew that every single employee in the company knew what was going on. For the first time ever the local weekly paper was nowhere to be seen in the canteen that week; the story was very prominent in the paper. Sometimes conversation would stop when I would enter a room, and of course I thought that everyone was talking about me. Nothing was said to me though and everyone was particularly kind to me during that time, which was almost unbearable. I felt so ashamed.

Both of my brothers naturally found the publicity of the case incredibly difficult to deal with, believing that their father's actions reflected more on them as men. Of course, this could not be further from the truth, but it was understandable that they might feel that way. My sister Marie and brother Alan were well settled in America and with no plans to return, we decided not to tell them anything of the court case.

And just when I thought things couldn't get any worse, Dad started drinking again. About a year after my parents moved to Tipperary, my father applied for a corporation house. They were given a two-bedroom terraced house the following year and soon after they moved in, Dad started drinking again. Mom hadn't wanted to move to a corporation house, but my father persuaded her, promising to finish the house to the highest standard with the best of furniture. He also pointed out that they would have more disposable income and more security, as they were getting older. So when Dad started drinking, Mom hit the roof and was having none of it. She insisted that he go for treatment this time. After his initial consultation in an addiction treatment centre, he was referred for a psychiatric assessment at the local hospital. The results showed that Dad had brain damage – most probably caused by his years of heavy drinking – and it was thought a full recovery was unlikely. Mom and I attended a meeting in the treatment centre, where we were told that because alcohol had suppressed Dad's emotional development for many years, his thinking had become quite distorted. The best we could hope for was sobriety. Mom said that sobriety would do.

Dad did stay sober for a couple of years although he was like Jeckel and Hyde the way his mood would change. Eventually his demons got the better of him and when he did start drinking again, he was worse than ever before and far more abusive. At this stage he was also taking prescription drugs as well (mainly Librium) and he became quite manic and obsessive in his behaviour. He left hateful notes around the house and was constantly starting rows, shouting obscenities and slamming doors. My mother had no peace with him and it wore her down. Mom had developed stress-related diverticulitis and had been in and out of hospital with increased frequency. Her doctor told her that the disease was most likely caused by stress and she certainly had a *lot* of that in her life! She decided to do something about Dad and this time she went to a solicitor for advice (there was another reason she wanted to separate from Dad and it concerned me, Sarah and Aunty Katie, but I'll explain that later). Mom obtained a barring order against her husband on the grounds of alcoholism, verbal abuse and Mom's failing health. My two brothers and I went to court with her and I testified to my father's abusive behaviour. Having a corporation house became a great advantage to Mom in the end – she could survive financially on her own now as her rent was means-tested (and was therefore very manageable) and she had her pension too. This made it so much easier for her to take action, which she did, even with her failing health.

Mom became legally separated from Dad the following year. She was seventy-five. I remember the judge saying that she was the oldest (he may have said 'most mature') person that he had ever granted a separation to. She called her sister Katie to tell her, believing that she had finally put things right and was hoping that they could begin again. Katie was all she had of her own family and I knew how much she had missed her in the years after Dad's trial. Unfortunately, she received a frosty reception and was bitterly disappointed and saddened by Katie's apparent indifference. As for myself, I was very proud of her and told her so. She had taken a stand and had shown tremendous courage. She did it for me, for Sarah and for her broken family. Most importantly, and probably for the first time in her life, Mom had done something for herself. She continued living in her small corporation house, which she was able to manage and she had some great neighbours, who kept an eye on her too. Even so, her medical condition and unfortunately her quality of life continued to deteriorate slowly after that.

Much has happened in my own life since my twenty-second birthday. It was quite a few a few more years before I found my way...

After a few months passed I began to go out with my brother to the local pub. I didn't know anyone in the town, but soon made friends, although most of them were guys. I also went swimming most nights, which I found very relaxing. I got a secretarial job in the office of a local manufacturing company and all seemed well.

But underneath the surface, I was still, naturally, deeply troubled. I began to go out more often – up to four or five nights a week and I usually drank too much. I was also behaving recklessly again, staggering home drunk or ending up in a strange bed with someone I hardly knew. I woke up one morning in a house in the middle of nowhere. The guy I had picked up had left for work and I had no idea where I was or how I would get home. I had to thumb a lift from a truck-driver and walk up the town before arriving home to the wrath of my mother. I felt this awful shame as I realised that things were getting out of hand. I decided that I would have to tone it down, and so I began to limit my nights out and got back into the weeknight swimming routine.

Then I met a guy called Kevin and he didn't drink at all. I thought this was just what I needed – someone sensible who didn't drink and I was delighted with myself. How very naïve of me. What I was soon to find out was that Kevin was a drinker who had stopped drinking and was therefore, a 'recovering alcoholic.' There's nothing wrong with that in itself, but I soon found out that Kevin was also cross-addicted, meaning he had more than one addiction. He gambled, and he hadn't stopped doing that! I didn't see what a hold it had over him until I was living with him.

Kevin wasn't capable of showing love or affection and he only ever appeared happy on his way to a race meeting. His story was heart-breaking – another unhappy childhood – only his was a particularly violent one. He opened up to me about being beaten throughout his childhood by his father, always after he came home from the pub full of whiskey. He told me that he jumped out the window one night to avoid a beating and broke his leg. Kevin was a very emotionally damaged person. I wanted to help him but didn't know how and I soon learned that he wouldn't let me anyway. I spent four years in this lonely relationship, starved of love or affection. I attempted to leave on a couple of occasions, but he became very aggressive and threatening, so I stayed. I remember lying awake in bed one night, with Kevin asleep beside me, and I felt like the loneliest person in the world. I felt so trapped and the question that baffled me the most was how had I ended up in a relationship with someone who was like my father in many ways?

One Saturday morning I told Kevin I was going away for the night. I had arranged a trip to Cork with my friend Helen, who was from Kinsale and was going home for the weekend. I was really looking forward to the break, as I never went away on my own. Kevin had lost a lot of money gambling and was now in serious debt – and not for the first time. I was packing my clothes and toiletries, when he started a row. He didn't trust me or believe me and said if I went, I needn't come back. I was determined his bully tactics weren't going to work this time, so I ignored him and continued packing. Kevin picked up the bag I was packing, walked out the front door, and threw it on the footpath outside our apartment. My clothes scattered everywhere. He came back inside, grabbed a bundle of clothes out of the wardrobe and threw them out on the path. He continued doing this until everything I owned was piled on the ground, outside our home, while he ranted and raved. He was in such a rage, his face was purple and his hands were shaking! I was hysterical. There were people and cars passing and looking on as I ran around, trying to pick everything up. I called Helen, who lived nearby, and thankfully she came straight over. We piled everything into the back of her car and went to her house. Once I had calmed down after a cup of tea and a cigarette, we sorted my stuff out and I packed an overnight bag.

We went to Kinsale and had a lovely time. Helen's family was very friendly and we had a lovely home-cooked dinner, followed by a walk around the harbour. Helen said I could stay with her until I got a place of my own. What had happened was horrible and not at all how I planned to leave, but at least I was free of Kevin now. He had blown it this time for good and I felt nothing but relief. I had been lonely and unhappy for so long and any love that I had for him was well gone. Within a week I moved in with Rita, another friend who, with her boyfriend Denis, had just finished building a house in the town. They were moving in downstairs and there were two rooms to rent upstairs. It was bright, spacious and central to the town and I settled in quickly.

All was well again, but not for long. Kevin called, crying, apologising and promising to change. He begged me to have dinner with him and because I felt sorry for him I went. He then begged me to go back to his place and because I felt sorry for him, I did. He wanted to have sex. I told him it was over, but I let him persuade me, even though I really did not want to. He knew that I was very different afterwards and it finally seemed to dawn on him that it was over between us. I didn't know it was possible to think less of myself at the time, but I hit a new low that night. Deep down, I really despised myself.

My 'rebound' was a guy in work called Simon, an engineer who I found myself very attracted to. Simon was just a nice person: serious, but kind, tall and strong – I just felt safe around him. We usually only met in the canteen or at meetings, so I didn't even know him very well. There was the obligatory office night out before Christmas that same year and I had a fling with him. I needed to have closure with Kevin and this was the only way I knew how, at the time. After six years of sobriety (although that was debatable) Kevin had started drinking again after our last night together. He had been calling me and when I stopped taking his calls, he began calling the office. When I refused to take his calls at work, he showed up in reception one day, drunk and aggressive. Once again, I was horribly embarrassed, something that seemed to happen often in my life, but something that I had never become used to. I was shocked, too, as I'd never seen Kevin drunk before. Thankfully, one of my colleagues dealt with him and he left.

Just before we broke up for Christmas, I heard Simon had got a new job in Dublin and would be leaving in January. Christmas came and went and before I knew it, Simon's 'leaving party' was on. I ended up spending the night with him once again. It was just sex with Simon: I knew that he didn't care about me and I didn't really care about him. I also realised that I didn't enjoy casual, drunken sex – I never had – and I didn't want to return to that in my life. More importantly, I wondered why I had been having casual sex all my life, when I didn't enjoy it. It left me feeling lonely and empty afterwards – and worthless too. There was a pattern in my behaviour that I hadn't seen before: I was drawn to having sex with men who I had no relationship with and relationships with men who were emotionally damaged and incapable of love. Neither made me happy and I knew that there had to be some underlying reason – I just didn't know what it was. I was also beginning to see that I had very low self-esteem and I wanted to do something about it; I wanted to change.

Six weeks passed after Simon left and I felt quite unwell. I was tired and nauseous all the time. I didn't know what was wrong with me so I made an appointment to see my doctor. I hadn't had a period in ages, but this was nothing unusual for me. I didn't get my first period until I was nineteen and they had been very irregular since, only getting two or three a year. I had been referred to a gynaecologist when I was about twenty and I was told that it was unlikely for me to conceive. I was to go for a follow-up appointment the following year, but never went. So when my doctor asked me if I had taken a pregnancy test, I told her that I didn't think I could be pregnant! Needless to say, I was very wrong. I *was* pregnant and with Simon's baby – someone I hardly knew. I didn't even have a contact number for him. I knew where he was from and the townland where his family lived, but that was all. I cried in my doctor's office that day. What was I going to do? I felt afraid, alone and completely out of my depth. How was I going to look after a baby when I wasn't even capable of taking care of myself? I couldn't even afford a car on my salary, never mind a baby! I didn't consider abortion or adoption as options for me, and I decided to take it one day at a time and try to get through the pregnancy as best I could.

I hadn't seen or heard from Kevin since the day he arrived at my office in a state, but as it happened, everyone – including my family and his – assumed that he was the father. Worse still, I didn't deny it (not intentionally at first), but the longer I left it, the harder it became. Nobody knew about Simon and I simply didn't have the strength of character to tell the truth at the time. I was already pretty overwhelmed with being pregnant! I suppose I was afraid I would be judged, especially by my family. I hadn't intended to lie: I just kept putting off telling the truth! Simon was quite a bit younger than me and was very focussed on his career and I thought he'd have no interest in having a child (that's what I told myself anyway). Kevin was probably a lost cause now that he was drinking again, so I wasn't sure what to do, but telling it straight didn't seem to make sense to me at the time. Oh, what a tangled web we weave...

My baby was due in October that year; I was twenty-eight years old and being a mother was not something I had ever considered in my life before. I found the pregnancy endless and was permanently nauseous and tired. I was also very frightened about the whole thing. I decided to move home as soon as my maternity leave started. It sounds crazy to me now to have considered moving back in with Mom and Dad, but it felt like it was the only option open to me at the time. I couldn't stay where I was, as Rita and Denis had other lodgers and besides, I had to start saving money for all the things the baby would need. I also needed to save up for a car if I was to continue working after my baby was born.

The next year was very challenging. David finally arrived after an endless pregnancy. I was left go a full two weeks over my due date and was hospitalized for those two weeks as the baby was breach. In the end, I had to be induced twice and have my waters broken before I went into a very fast and painful labour. It was all worth it in the end: David was a beautiful, healthy child and I was very relieved and very grateful. He was so quiet in the hospital and slept most of the time – it must have been a traumatic experience for him too. David wasn't quiet for long though – the day I brought him home he started screaming and he didn't stop for almost fourteen months! I called the CareDoc in the middle of the first night when I couldn't settle him – it sounded like he was in serious pain – and I panicked. There was nothing the doctor could find wrong and said he was probably a bit colicky.

David's first year of life was a total blur. He had severe colic, was milk-intolerant and had numerous chest infections, twice needing to be hospitalised because of breathing difficulties. The poor baby didn't cry like other babies: he screamed constantly from about four o'clock every afternoon until about four or five the following morning. He never slept for more than a couple of hours at a time and that was always during the day. I went back to work after my maternity leave ended, having found a good day-care centre nearby. I walked to work and back every day, leaving David in the nursery, often after only an hour's sleep. Then I faced into a hectic day in a busy sales office, usually falling asleep at the desk after I'd eaten my lunch.

I became more and more tired as the weeks and months went by. The nights were so tough. I shared a room with David and could do nothing for him but hold him and rub his stomach and back as he cried inconsolably for hours on end. Then I would hear my father giving out to Mom about the 'awful racket' and saying that we'd have to move out because he needed his sleep. I would wait for my parents to go to bed and then bring David downstairs so his crying wouldn't be as loud. It was all very stressful. One night, demented with tiredness and frustration, I purposely hit my head against the wall, nearly knocking myself out! I lay down on the bed, dazed and shocked, before crying into my pillow. *At least it was my head and not David's*, I thought to myself, but the thought frightened me; I knew I was beginning to unravel. Sometimes I lost control and shouted at David, or put the pillow over my head and tried to block out the noise – a noise that I couldn't do anything to stop. David's screaming made me feel utterly useless as a mother. I felt so helpless that I couldn't do anything for his pain and it made me feel like a complete failure.

Kevin called one day to tell me that a friend of his, Frank (a fellow gambler whom I had met on occasion at various race-meetings), had committed suicide. Frank was a young farmer from Tipperary who was well-mannered but quiet, shy even. He didn't seem like the gambling type to me at all. Kevin and he often went to race-meetings together and both of them got involved in late night poker games too. Kevin was obviously shaken to his very core. He explained how they had been to the races together two days previously and both had lost money. Frank said he was going to go home, but went instead to an all-night casino in Cork, where he lost everything. He then drove to the coast, wrote a letter to his parents – which he left in his car – and walked out into the sea, fully clothed. Frank couldn't swim and the sea took him. It was winter and the thought of poor Frank, wading out into the sea brought tears to my eyes. Kevin had been involved in the search and his body had been found that morning.

Kevin decided shortly after Frank was buried to get help and he checked himself into Aisiri, the same treatment centre that Dad had attended. I went to a couple of the family days to help and support him, but made it quite clear that there would be no reconciliation between us. It was my fourth time attending Aisiri and I hoped it would be my last. I could have given the presentation on addiction; I had heard it so many times!

Home was miserable for me as Dad was constantly giving out and it was just making things tougher for Mom. Eventually I became ill myself, having three consecutive bouts of tonsillitis in as many months and was really unwell each time. I was run down and completely sleep deprived, so it was hardly surprising. One morning I woke up and began crying inconsolably. I didn't know why I was crying or what was wrong with me and I couldn't stop. I went to my doctor who was seeing me fairly regularly at this stage. She told me that she thought it most likely that I was depressed, given my symptoms and all that was going on. She did some blood tests as we talked about my options, of which there were two: I could either take medication or I could go for counselling. There was no way I was going to take anti-depressants – not if there was another way – so I told her I would go for counselling. My doctor took out her diary and gave me the name of a counsellor who she said was very good, and reasonably priced too. She let me call, there and then in her office, and I made the appointment for the following week. She then gave me a sick cert and told me to come back if I needed to take a further week.

I will always be grateful to my doctor for showing me such kindness and for helping me at a time when I felt completely overwhelmed by my life. She was very understanding and genuinely concerned. Before I left her office, I asked if there was a tonic or supplement I could take – something to give me more energy again. I will never forget her response:

'Deirdre,' she said, 'what you need doesn't come in a bottle unfortunately. You need a lifestyle change. You're running yourself into the ground and the depression is your body's way of telling you that something has to give. Maybe you might think about getting a part-time job until David is a little older? You might be entitled to a supplementary payment as a single parent. It's something that might be worth looking into.'

It was the best advice she could have given me and I knew she was right. Why hadn't I thought of it before? I would start looking for a part-time job straight away. I was beginning to feel so much better already.

Counselling was the best thing that ever happened to me, although it did take some time. The first counsellor, the one that my doctor referred me to, was a man by the name of John. He was a lovely person: very kind and gentle in his manner. He explained a lot to me about dysfunctional families and co-dependency and I learned a lot from him. After a few months, John told me he was putting together a small group of women with similar issues for a group therapy session and asked if I would be interested in taking part. I said I would and found myself sitting in his therapy room one night with three other women of varying ages. Working with a group seemed to accelerate and intensify everything. I could relate to what the others were saying and we were supportive and understanding of each other. I got on particularly well with a woman called Marian, and we became very good friends in time.

One night John told us that we were going to do some 'inner child' work, through the use of a regression-style meditation developed by John Bradshaw, who John said was a very well-known American psychologist, specialising in this kind of work. He explained that we would be regressed back to our childhoods during the meditation, where we would have the opportunity to reclaim something significant from our childhood and bring it back to the present. It all sounded very positive, but as I went back, I became quite fearful. When I was asked to look around, I found Coco, my yellow childhood teddy bear, who I had no memory of whatsoever until that moment. I felt instant pain, anguish and confusion. Coco was my best friend in the world; how could I have forgotten him and where did he go? I became so overwhelmed with sadness and grief that John had to stop the session. I remember going home that night feeling incredibly lonely. I felt this huge loss for Coco, which I couldn't understand at the time. He was only a teddy – I kept saying to myself – how could I be feeling such pain over a teddy? That night I curled up in bed and cried myself to sleep.

By this time, I had moved out and was renting a two bed-roomed terraced house in the town, which was dry at least, even if it was a bit dark and dingy. There was no garden in Martin Street and no light either, but the rent was cheap and at least I was independent of my family and standing on my own two feet, which was priceless! I was very glad we moved because Dad was drinking again, blaming me and the baby this time! David had just turned one, and his nightly bouts of colic were beginning to get shorter. He was just starting to walk and I was really enjoying his company and his love for me.

After another couple of sessions with John, he suggested that I go to a different counsellor, a woman by the name of Mary. He believed that I would make more progress seeing a woman as he felt I had some trust issues with men and that he had done as much work with me as I would allow. John said I had worked very hard, but in order for me to continue to work through my issues I needed to feel completely safe. He was right: I didn't feel completely safe with any man at that time and John had made a wise suggestion. I started seeing Mary the following week and, thankfully, just continued from where I left off with John. I liked Mary instantly: she was warm, friendly and very easy to talk to. She also had a wonderful sense of humour and helped me to laugh a little more and see the humour in things. I really enjoyed our sessions together and quickly grew to trust her.

Mary explained to me that emotions were like the layers of an onion. When we acknowledge and express one emotion, there is usually another waiting to be revealed underneath. Sadness and grief often come after anger and hurt, and sometimes it's the reverse. We are all different in the way we work through our feelings. What is important is to keep working through all the layers and not to let fear get in the way. Mary also explained how Coco, my teddy, represented all of the loss and grief I had experienced in my own childhood. He had also been my confidante and possibly the only one that I opened up to and shared my secrets with. Coco had also been my hero (albeit inadvertently), as finding him was like finding a key to unlocking my past.

I was beginning to understand so much about myself and the other people in my life. I had been going around in circles, making the same mistakes repeatedly and was causing myself so much more pain in the process. I could now see the benefits of taking the time to undo the past and the negative thinking patterns and beliefs that came from my unhappy childhood. What's more, a very beautiful thing was happening: I was beginning to get to know myself better and I liked who I was becoming. I stopped blaming myself and being hard on myself all the time. I began to see that what other people did or said was because of the way they were, not because of me. Mary helped me to understand that I didn't have to take it all personally and that what others did was their responsibility, not mine. My only responsibility was to owning my own feelings in relation to everyone and everything and processing those feelings. I also had to take responsibilities for my actions, decisions and behaviour. I was slowly learning to trust myself and to care for myself too.

One of the hardest parts of the counselling process for me was acknowledging the hurt that my father had caused me and also to grieve for the father that I wished I had – the Dad of my dreams (who possibly looked a lot like Tom Selleck!). I needed to do this or else the cycle would have continued and I would have always been drawn to emotionally damaged people – like my father. My boyfriends (as I found out) had just been different versions of my father, so how could those relationships have worked out? Mary explained to me that this was very typical: that I had not consciously tried to replicate the relationship I had with my Dad, but I was drawn to what had not been healed in that relationship – what I couldn't fix – and there was plenty of that! I was also subconsciously drawn to what I knew, what was familiar, whether I liked it or not. I needed to learn to accept my father as he was and let go of the father that he was not, nor could ever be. Mary said, 'Remember that your inner child may be looking for a father, but the adult in you is looking for an intimate friend and sexual partner. The two don't go together, Dee!'

This made sense to me, but I was afraid that there would be this big gaping hole inside, that the emptiness and loneliness would be unbearable. In hindsight, what I was really afraid of was change – of letting go. What was familiar to me may have been miserable, but it was what I knew. I was heading into uncharted waters and I didn't know what to expect.

What was causing my great confusion around my father was the issue of sexual abuse. I knew that I had been emotionally and socially abandoned by my Dad at quite a young age – maybe six or seven – but the biggest problem was that I had so few memories....

I knew for sure that my father had sexually abused both my cousins and my best friend's sister Ann. Everything pointed to having been abused by him at a young age: the inappropriate play with my cousin (and with myself), the nightmares, remembering how his voice would change, the sick feelings in my stomach and the intense dislike of him growing up. Yet I didn't remember any specific incidents, other than being bounced up and down on his lap (and hating it), and I really struggled with this. I made up my mind that I was more comfortable with the term 'sexualised' – that my father had sexualised me as a child. I spent a session or two with Mary, working on the incident with my dad and Ann in the car, which I found really difficult. Firstly, I couldn't understand how I felt so much shame, guilt and confusion, even though I was just witnessing the abuse. It was as if it had happened to me. Mary explained that this was normal, too, that children at that age cannot differentiate between themselves and others, in terms of responsibility. Therefore, whatever is happening around them (from arguing to physical or sexual abuse) becomes their fault. Secondly, I felt huge guilt over not doing something to stop my father, that I had failed Ann in some way. Mary continued to reassure me that I was only a child and that this was my father. 'What could a seven-year-old have done?' she asked. 'If I were to tell you the story, about another seven-year-old in the same situation, would you expect her to be able to stop it?' I tried to take this on board, but I knew I hadn't completely let myself off the hook.

I had written a few letters to my father during counselling sessions (and sometimes as homework), telling him how I felt. Eventually, I mustered up enough courage to face him – something I decided I had to do. The plan was to write a letter and read it to him. That way, I could be sure not to forget anything that I needed to say. I was prepared for him to try to walk away; Dad never listened to what he didn't want to hear and I was prepared for his denial. I called Mom and told her that I needed to talk to Dad and would be calling to the house to see him. It turned out to be more difficult than I had imagined. I had to follow him around the house, and even stopped him from leaving by blocking the front door, until I was finished. He called me a liar and said I was talking rubbish. It didn't matter what he said – I had spoken my truth and I didn't let him stop me. I pushed the letter into his hand when I was finished.

'You know the truth,' I said. 'You just won't admit it.'

I walked out the front door, shaking from head to toe. The minute I sat into my car, I started to cry uncontrollably; I was crying with sheer relief. I also felt a sense of achievement I had never felt before. Standing up for myself, and for everyone else that I knew my father had abused was very liberating. I had begun the process of taking my power back and it felt good.

My father went into the blackest of moods after this and unfortunately Mom and Jack (who was now living with them) took the brunt of it. I felt guilty, but Mary said I had nothing to feel guilty about – that I had to put myself first and speak my truth. I talked to Mom on the phone (as I didn't want to call to the house for a while), and I told her that she didn't have to take it either – that she had choices too. That was when she decided to go and see a solicitor to see what options she had. She was told she could apply for a legal separation, which would take at least one year. The solicitor also advised Mom to apply to the court for a barring order while she waited for her separation, saying that her husband's behaviour was abusive and threatening. Mom got the barring order and I was very proud of her. She really didn't find it easy, going down to the courthouse with her solicitor, but she did it.

So why was I feeling so depressed a few weeks later? I even forgot my next appointment with Mary, which was something I never did. Then I realised I was letting fear get the better of me and I knew I had to dig a little deeper and find a bit more courage to see where this new road was taking me. I knew I still had lots of work to do.

I started to go to mass again, and although I had many conflicting views about the Catholic Church I was willing to explore them. I knew that I was a spiritual human being, that there was a bigger part of me that I wanted to tap into again. I didn't need to be a devout, unquestioning Catholic to enjoy mass, and I didn't have to agree with the church about everything either: it was essentially man-made and therefore flawed, just like me. The quality of my life was improving mainly down to the fact that I had a new job, working part-time as a merchandiser for a cigarette company. The hours suited me, the money was good and I got to spend more time with David. I even passed my driving test and got my first full driving license. Working part-time also gave me the opportunity to take a little time to myself and I often found myself in a church somewhere, lighting a candle and talking to God, even if it was just for ten minutes.

David and I spent most weekends in Marian's; she had also started to go to Mary for counselling and we were a great support for one another. Marian was renting a lovely house in an estate that sat on a hill, overlooking the town. It was tastefully decorated, bright and cosy. She had been living there with her boyfriend, who she broke up with shortly after beginning counselling. Marian and I spent many nights talking and laughing as we listened to music or watched a film. We rarely went out at weekends, preferring to get a take-away and a bottle of wine. We often had our own little disco in the sitting room as we both loved to dance. My world began to feel safe again. I was making better decisions for myself and for my son. Six months passed and with it, David's second birthday and he was doing great. He was even sleeping right through the night now and was a happy and loving child. The merchandising job was going very well as were my counselling sessions with Mary.

Winter came and I found the weeknights long and lonely once David went to bed. One night I sat in front of the fire and cried bitterly; I felt such despair. My life had been so miserable really. I had never been nurtured, or listened to. I had felt so unloved growing up and now I was living in a miserable, dingy townhouse with nobody to talk to at night and I felt very lonely. It wasn't long before despair kicked in as I wondered if my life was ever going to get better. It was as if I had just fallen down a hole into a bottomless pit! I cancelled two appointments with Mary and she eventually called me to see if I was okay. I explained that I was very down: that I felt like I had a mountain to climb and had just fallen into a big, dark hole. We rescheduled the session again for the middle of January. Then Mary said something that helped me to get up and go again.

'Don't quit now Dee. You're so close and you've worked so hard. Believe me, it will all be worth it.'

Shortly after that I got some great news. Marian was in the process of buying a small house where she was also going to set up a therapy practice (she was a massage therapist), and she asked me if I'd be interested in taking the house that she had been renting. She had already spoken to the landlord and he had no objections. I was delighted and happily gave my notice in Martin Street. I could afford the rent and Marian's place was already home from home, for both David and me, which would make the move easier. We moved into our new home just before my thirtieth birthday in January. The estate agent had just given Marian the keys to her new home too and she was like a child on Christmas morning. She was also delighted for us to be moving from our dingy little flat into a lovely bright spacious new home. It came at just the right time too. Our lovely new environment gave me the lift that I needed to take the next step and what a great start it was to the New Year.

David loved his big, bright room and having a front and back garden made him even more excited. There had been very little stability in David's little life as we had moved house four times since he was born and I was acutely aware this. I longed for more security in our lives, for both our sakes, but I knew that I was doing my best under difficult circumstances. I was managing my life and my time well and I had found balance in my life for the first time. I was a good mother and a good friend and all of these things were helping me to believe in myself again and ultimately to trust myself again. I wasn't perfect, but as Mary constantly reminded me, I didn't have to be. I just needed to be patient, something I had never been very good at!

My life seemed to have a flow to it now, a certain symmetry that allowed me to continue to move forward. What had been blocking me before Christmas was letting go of the father that I didn't have and the loss and grief that came with that. It was a huge task and I could see, in hindsight, why I had hit a wall. I needed to feel safer and more secure, and I did now, in my lovely new home. I knew now that I could do the letting go here. Saying what I had to say to my father had empowered me greatly. I expressed my feelings, my anger and my hurt – the truth as I remembered it. Mary asked me not to focus on trying to remember something: instead we would concentrate on connecting with how I felt. She explained that young children cannot often put words on experiences, especially ones they don't understand.

'Children just feel their feelings,' Mary said, 'and that's all you need to be willing to do – to allow your little girl to feel and express her feelings.' So using a photograph of myself as a child, I allowed myself to go there: to a deep, dark place within myself. With my eyes closed, and using a lump of clay as a means of helping me, I finally let go and allowed my feelings guide me. It was an incredibly difficult process. I could feel my father poke and prod and invade me, body and soul. I felt such confusion, such anger and betrayal. I also felt so hurt and so violated. My father had turned my young, innocent world into such a nightmare, that I never knew what it was like to feel normal. The pain was so intense, I could hardly breathe. The poisonous nausea and shame that I always took responsibility for was clearly not mine and never had been. It became obvious as I worked with the clay that my father couldn't have hurt me more deeply if he had taken my life and I cried myself inside out. There was so much hurt inside me, I thought I might die.

Marian called up that night after David went to bed and just held me. I cried like the hurt child that I was. I wailed and sobbed and cried like I never had before; it was endless. Eventually, the tears stopped and I felt empty and exhausted. I thanked Marian for being there for me and for being so supportive. When she left, I crawled into bed and slept until David woke me the following morning. It was a lovely bright day and as I didn't have work, David and I had a bath together and went for a walk. As my mind cleared and I breathed in the fresh morning air, I realised that I felt better than I had ever remembered feeling in my life: so light, so free, and so very strong. I felt like I had just climbed a mountain and was savouring the view. I decided that David and I would have a fun day so we went to the playground, followed by McDonald's, and then out to the lake to feed the swans. We had a really lovely nurturing day.

Mary suggested, during one of our sessions, that I go away by myself for a night or two, maybe somewhere I had never been before and to treat it as an adventure. So that spring Mom took David for the weekend and off I went. My boss told me of a beautiful place in County Clare called Kilkee, and that's where I headed. It was my first break away from David and I was going to make the most of having time to myself. It sounded perfect too: a pretty village right beside the sea, with lovely cliff walks and breathtaking views. I didn't book anything – I just packed a bag and off I went. I felt as free as a bird and was excited about having my very own adventure. I loved the sea and missed living close to it, as I had in Dublin, so I was really looking forward to spending time on the west coast.

I wasn't disappointed – Kilkee was everything I thought it would be and more. I stayed in a lovely guesthouse with a wonderful restaurant attached, overlooking Kilkee bay. My room was warm and homely with big bay windows and stunning sea views. The owners were friendly and welcoming too. It was perfect and just what I needed. I brought my diary and did some writing in the evenings. What I really enjoyed was the sea, and I spent hours walking and stopping along the cliff tops, looking out at the sea and breathing in the wonderful energy of the Atlantic. I may have been alone, but for the first time in my life I didn't feel lonely. I saw the sun setting over the ocean, in a kaleidoscope of colour and it was breathtaking. It was good to be alive!

Just before I left on the Sunday, something compelled me to drive to one of the car parks at the edge of the village and I walked out to the edge of the cliff one last time. I looked out over the ocean and to my amazement I saw a school of dolphins swimming near the shore. It was so beautiful my eyes filled up with tears. I had never seen dolphins in their natural environment before and to be so close to them was very special. I felt it was just for me. I stayed there, transfixed for nearly an hour and others gathered around to watch the dolphins playing too. I felt so connected in that moment to God and to nature and I quietly gave thanks for this magical place, for my life and for everything. My weekend in Kilkee had affected me profoundly and for the first time in my life, I felt like I belonged – to myself and to this beautiful planet. I felt like I had come home to myself and I didn't need anyone else to feel whole or complete: I had me. The dolphins were the perfect end to a perfect weekend.

My life had new possibilities, and I was full of hope for my future and the future of my son. There was nothing I couldn't handle now. I felt so much stronger. I decided to deal with some of the skeletons that were still hanging in my closet when I got back to Tipperary! I had been worried about having a sexually transmitted disease ever since the night I was raped (and also because I had unprotected sex a few times as well), so I went to a STD clinic on Mary's advice and had full blood tests done. Thankfully, everything came back clear. I was incredibly relieved as it was something that I had pushed to the back of my mind for a long time. Then there was David. I didn't feel ready to deal with the whole father issue yet, but I did want to have him baptized and had put it off so many times because I hadn't come clean as to who his father was. I decided to talk to one of my local parish priests. I dropped David down to my mother's and walked down to the church. There was a terrace of three small houses alongside the church, which were the homes of the three priests in the parish. I didn't know which was which but was hoping I would get the younger priest as I thought he would be easier to talk to. I knocked on the first door, but there was no answer. I knocked on the second door and, as it opened, my heart sank; it was the older priest. I was very nervous as I asked him if I could talk to him about a personal issue. He invited me in and was so warm and kind, I began to relax. I told him about David and how I had messed things up. I explained that I had not told the truth as to who his real father was and that I wanted to have him baptized but didn't want to lie before God. I could scarcely believe that the words had come out of my mouth and I waited to be chastised and told what a terrible person I was.

I wasn't prepared for what this small, frail old man said to me. 'I can see that you are very upset about this and that you didn't intend for this to happen,' he said. 'And if I can see that, God can see it too. I'm sure that you will put this situation right when you are ready to. In the meantime, get your little boy baptized and stop worrying.' He then added with a warm smile, 'You haven't murdered anyone, have you?'

I was so grateful I nearly shook his hand right off and I must have thanked him ten times before I left. I floated home that day, such was the relief that I felt. I thanked God in his wisdom for bringing me to the right person at the right time, and I reminded myself (not for the first time) not to have preconceptions about people. I arranged for David to be baptized soon after. It was a lovely spring day and for me, finally, it was an opportunity to celebrate my son's birth. He was gifted to me and I was so grateful to have him in my life. My son loved me unconditionally and gave me a purpose and a focus in my life. I promised myself (and David) that I would put things right and asked God to help me.

Life moved forward and David went to playschool the following autumn. Kevin had managed to stay sober and had stopped gambling and he sometimes picked David up and brought him to the playground, or to the cinema. Of course I felt very guilty at times: Kevin still thought he was David's father and I didn't know how to tell him otherwise yet. I could see that he was so damaged inside and was like a child himself in many ways. I managed to persuade Kevin to go to Mary for counselling, when he started gambling again. Kevin surprisingly agreed to go and told Mary about the beatings by his father, adding that his father didn't know any better. Mary disagreed with him, saying that his father knew that what he was doing was wrong. With that, Kevin jumped up, said, 'I've got what I needed here. How much do I owe you Mary?' With that he went straight to his parent's house and beat his father to the ground in a rage, stating that it was the best therapy he ever had! He regretted it afterwards, but he never went back to counselling again.

Winter came and went and the following spring my life took another turn. The cigarette company that I worked for were putting together a new sales team, with excellent training and career prospects. As an existing employee, I was entitled to an interview which I wouldn't have got otherwise, as all external applicants had to be college graduates. I really wanted to own my own home and have some financial security, something I desperately wanted for David also. I got the job and with it a new company car, a laptop and a phone. I was thrilled! I was told that after the six-month training period that there would be five full-time positions available. Only one of these would be in the Tipperary/Kilkenny area, where I wanted to be based. The others would be Dublin and the West. I had to be the best of the six candidates to have the first choice of location.

I explained everything to David as best I could about why I was not going to be around as much and he was so brave. I worked so hard over the next six months and only saw David on weekends, which was heartbreaking. Mom and Kevin looked after him and I know it must have been tough on David. I don't think I realised at the time how much of a sacrifice it was for him. I got home as early as I could on Fridays and left as late as I could every Sunday night. Being away from my son motivated me all the more. I was the first up in the morning and the last one home. I always pushed myself to make one more call, and it paid off. I came out as the best candidate with the best sales and was offered the choice of locations. I chose the southeast, which meant I could base myself locally enough and be in a position to put a deposit on a house within the year. Everything was going to plan, but then the unexpected happened: one of the Dublin sales reps decided to look for a transfer to my area and, as he was with the company longer, he was entitled to swipe it from under my nose. I was really devastated – after all my hard work. This left me with only two options, Mayo or Dublin. Mayo was just too far away from friends and family, and maybe I had unfinished business in Dublin, given that I had run away from my life there before. Very reluctantly, I chose to return to the city I hadn't lived in for over a decade. I only hoped it wouldn't be for too long: most of the reps in the south were nearing retirement, so anything was possible.

The company helped me to find a house to rent in my region, which ran from west Dublin up to Ballyfermot and east into Dublin City. I settled on a bungalow in Knocklyon. I was completely unfamiliar with this part of Dublin and it felt a million miles away from the place that I knew and grew up in. I found a good day-care centre for David, which was very close to where we were to live. Both my rent and day-care costs were outrageously expensive, and even with my good salary the prospect of buying a house seemed further away again. I would be lucky to make ends meet, living in Dublin. David, who was three and a half, found the transition very difficult. He had been taken away from his grandma and Uncle Jack and everything else that was familiar. Now there was just the two of us in a big city suburb with no friends or family and we were both feeling it. David also had to adjust to full-time day-care in a whole new environment, which we both found very tough. He had to be peeled from my arms every morning for the first two weeks – it was almost unbearable. After agonising over whether I was doing the right thing, I would compose myself and focus on the day's work, which was tough going at the best of times. I would get all my calls done, without stopping to eat most days so that I could get back to pick David up, usually before four o'clock. We had a few hours before bedtime to play and spend time together. Then I would go back to work, processing my orders and paperwork until ten or eleven every night. I never had time to contact old friends and we went home to Tipperary most weekends.

This went on for two years and the long days and nights were beginning to take their toll. I was doing very well in the job, but the workload was huge and I was becoming tired and run-down. I was constantly getting chest infections and having to take antibiotics, but I just kept going, not knowing what else to do. I had stopped seeing Mary too and I was missing her support. September came and time for David to start school. I was dreading it as the local primary school was one of the biggest schools in the country and I knew it would be challenging for David. I took a week off work so that I could bring him to school every morning and collect him every day. He found it all very overwhelming at first, but he did eventually settle in. The day-care centre had a minibus and did the local school runs, so I continued to drop David there every morning and they would then bring him to school and collect him every day. I made sure I was finished in time to collect him every Friday. I wished I could have collected him every day and I felt very guilty at times; I was beginning to see what a high price I was paying for the dream of having our own home.

David was getting older and as we became closer, I was becoming acutely aware of the deceit that I had created between us. He was a wonderful child and he deserved the truth. I decided it was time to put things right regarding his birth father, Simon. I managed to get through to Simon's father, after making a few phone calls in the general area where he lived. I told him I was an old friend of Simon's, but that I had lost his mobile number. He gave me Simon's number – I thanked him and quickly hung up. My heart started to beat very fast and I decided I would call him straight away before I lost my nerve. I noticed that my hands were shaking as I dialled the number. The phone rang and I took a deep breath and asked God to guide me. I wasn't even certain I had the right person until he answered; I recognized his voice straight away.

'Simon, you probably don't remember me – we worked together in Merlo's.' He assured me that he did remember me and then asked, 'what can I do for you Deirdre?' I knew he was on his guard and could hear from his voice that he was a little anxious.

'There's something I have to tell you, Simon, and it's going to come as a bit of a shock. There's no easy way to say this,' I said nervously . . . 'you have a son, David. He's five now.'

Silence followed. God knows what Simon was thinking, but he must have been very shocked. He then told me that he was in a serious relationship and wanted to discuss this with his girlfriend before he did anything else. When he called me back a few days later, Simon first insisted on a DNA test before we took things any further. I understood his concerns completely and it took a few more weeks to get through that process. Then we arranged to meet the following weekend in Tipperary and I explained everything to him. I asked him to think about whether he wanted to be a part of David's life and if so, he would have to make a real commitment to him and not let him down. Simon naturally asked me why I had left it so long before telling him. I knew I had to tell him the truth, so I did, explaining that I didn't have the strength of character at the time to do the right thing. I told him about my depression and subsequent counselling and I apologised for not contacting him sooner. I said I was really sorry and that I could not change the past, no matter how much I wanted to. I was doing the right thing now – and I could do no more than that. Simon said that he would think about it and get back to me.

After meeting with Simon, I spoke to a very kind child therapist in Dublin and explained the situation to her regarding David. I needed advice as I wanted to be as honest with my son as I could be, without causing him undue confusion or upset. The therapist met with David twice and then gave me advice on how to handle things. She established that David hadn't bonded with Kevin as a father, and felt that he would get over it in time. She warned that he may have a bigger issue trusting me again – and to give this time and patience. She said to tell my son the truth, simply and honestly, which I did, with great difficulty. He took it very well, considering. There have been times since when he has found it difficult to trust me and has been very angry with me, but we have always talked these issues through and with a lot of patience, the trust has been restored again. Self-esteem was an issue for quite a few years for David, but in the last few years he has really matured and finally seems to value who he is. He has a reasonably good relationship with Simon: they see each other every couple of months and talk on the phone regularly too.

I also made the dreaded call to Kevin (who had stayed sober since his time in Aisiri) and met him to tell him that he was not David's father. It was one of the most difficult things I have ever had to do, as I was completely responsible for this situation and had deceived Kevin more than anyone in the process. Thankfully, he was very understanding and said he had known in his heart that he was not David's father, but I could see that he was still hurt. He said he would like to keep in touch with David, which he has. Kevin has never forgotten David at Christmas or his birthday and this means a lot to David. Thankfully, Kevin is happily married now and has a daughter of his own.

Simon came to meet David a few times in Knocklyon and those first meetings were naturally a bit awkward. Simon would bring a football or a couple of hurleys and a sliotar and they would play around on the local green. Soon they were heading off together and going to the cinema, or to the park and having a bite to eat out. I was happy with the way things were going with Simon and was glad that something good had come out of our move to Dublin, but that was the only thing that was going well. I wasn't happy with my job – my overheads were so high which didn't allow me to save any extra money – and we had no quality of life. I felt like I was getting nowhere and was burning myself out in the process. Thankfully, I received some good news on that front, which led me to make a decision about my future.

I had joined the share-save scheme when I first started working part-time with the company and had been paying into the scheme ever since. This was my first chance to buy shares or get a cash dividend. I chose the cash and got back nine thousand euro. This was my deposit on a house, but not in Dublin. I had no chance of buying there with the prices of houses and apartments. As I would not have another share option for three years. I decided to look for a transfer, on the grounds that I could not afford to live in Dublin any more. When I showed my boss the cost of renting and childcare alone, he could not argue with me. I worked hard for the company and knew they didn't want to lose me. I would have to forgo my sales position and take on a relief position, which would mean much more travelling as I would be covering holidays and sick-leave. However, it did mean that I could base myself back in Tipperary again, so I didn't care. At last I could start looking for a house! Dublin had served its purpose and I was stronger now and more self-reliant. I was also more confident. Another thing that was playing on my mind was my lack of job satisfaction. Although I was good at my job, I wasn't enjoying it anymore; the novelty of having the best sales figures every month had worn off. This job that took so much of my time and energy wasn't fulfilling me on a personal level anymore.

David and I continued to travel home every other weekend, although not having anywhere to stay made it quite stressful at times. Marian only had one bedroom, as she worked from home and used her other bedroom as an office. Jack was now living back with Mom and since Mom's house had only two bedrooms, we couldn't stay there. Sometimes we stayed with Marian (she had a big sofa!) and sometimes we stayed in a cheap bed and breakfast. The weekends that we stayed in Dublin, I tried to make fun for David. We'd go to Bray, Dun Laoghaire, Howth or Malahide, or mooch around the city, going to a show or exhibition. Only once did I get back in touch with one of my old friends, Donna. We called over to Clontarf, where she lived with her husband Jack and new baby, Barry. We spent a lovely sunny day with them. We went to Howth for a walk along the pier and it was lovely, but I felt like I was being scrutinised all the time (most likely in my own head). I felt the weight of my past, following my around, and it made me feel very uncomfortable and self-conscious. I also felt that I would never be able to keep up with their very comfortable lifestyles: they had plenty of money, ate in the best restaurants, shopped in the best boutiques and shops, while I was barely surviving financially. I had very little time and even less disposable income. I didn't get back in touch and neither did Donna. I think, more than anything, I just found it too hard to go back to anything that reminded me of my old life, or of who I used to be.

Mom's health was deteriorating and I was worried about her. Her diverticulitis was now acute and she had been in and out of hospital with increased frequency. I noticed too that she was losing weight and had become very confined by her condition. I remember the day I got the transfer finalised. I only had four weeks left in Dublin, which would bring us into July and then I could get out of Dublin. I called Mom to tell her and she was over the moon. The plan was to find somewhere cheap to rent while I looked for a house of my own. It also meant that David could start in a local school in September; I couldn't wait. I could see the relief on David's face when I told him; he was so happy to be going back home. We travelled down the following Friday as I had made an appointment with a mortgage consultant that Friday evening. Everything went great and he thought I would have no problem getting a mortgage for between ninety and one hundred thousand euro. I went to all the estate agents on Saturday morning, but there was nothing much in my price range and anything that I could afford needed quite a lot of work done. I didn't lose heart though – my search had just begun and I knew that I would find something soon.

We spent Sunday with Mom and didn't leave for Dublin until after seven o'clock. Mom stood at the door as we were leaving, as she always did. I told her that I loved her and gave her my usual hug and kiss goodbye. She looked into my eyes and said, 'and I *adore* you.' She gave David a big hug and told him she loved him too. My eyes welled up as I walked to the car – my mother had never spoken like that to me before and I was taken aback. Mom had often told me that she loved me (mostly as an adult), but this was different. I looked back at her in my rear-view mirror as she waved us off from her front door. It was to be the last time that she waved me off from her little red-bricked corporation house.

I thought about Mom and about our relationship on the way back to Dublin. David usually slept on the journey back and it was often a time that I got lost in my thoughts. Mom and I hadn't got on for most of my life, and she had spent much of it wrapped up in her life and her problems and I had become very wrapped up in mine. I tried to understand her, but never could. We were polar opposites really; I couldn't have been more unlike my mother if I tried. I also didn't feel that I understood her – she was the most complex person I knew. She could be cold and detached, childish and sulky, unreasonable and demanding – and then be kind and supportive, loving and generous. And all in the one day!

Mom never, ever spoke of her past: not her parents or her childhood and if anyone ever asked her any questions, it was clear that she didn't want to talk about it. The only interest she ever had that brought her joy was poker. She loved playing poker and set up a weekly classic in a local hotel not long after I arrived in Tipperary. It was a great success and before long there was a regular crowd going every Monday night and Mom was delighted with herself. She gave half the money out in prizes and half to charity. She never went outside the door without looking her best and she always dressed well.

Ever the lady, she always wore a nice skirt and blouse, or a smart suit on Sunday (for mass) or if she was going out. Mom had her hair done regularly, never went out without make-up (never too much – she was very conservative) and she always held her head high, no matter what was going on around her. Keeping a clean and tidy house was also very important to my mother: she dusted, polished, scrubbed, cleaned and vacuumed her home every week with regimental precision.

I knew that my mother loved me though, and she had always put a dinner on the table and a lunch in my bag going to school. She was good at the practical stuff, but not so good at being there in any emotional way for me growing up. She had downright neglected me emotionally when I was a child, but we had become closer in the last few years and I called her a few times a week for a chat. I usually got us all dinner in the take-away around the corner from Mom's on our way home on Friday, and we'd catch up on the news of the week.

I spoke to her on occasion about the past and how I felt about some of the things that happened, or about her parenting, especially during the time I was going to counselling. Mom would get defensive or teary-eyed and sometimes both, so I only challenged her when something was very important or when I really needed to get something off my chest. In counselling, Mary would often get me to imagine sitting my mother down in her armchair, where I could really let go with her and speak my mind (and I never had to deal with her response which was great!). Mary would often remind me that I wasn't responsible for my mother's happiness – something which took a long time to sink in!

The one thing Mom and I both loved was walking and nature and we had been going for walks since I was a teenager when we lived in Skerries. I especially remember going for long walks while I was pregnant with David. We'd talk about life and wonder what it was all about. Mom lived a life of wishing for what she didn't have in her life, wishing it had all been different, or that she had more money and I felt so sorry for her at times. I wished regularly too, mostly that if I had been more successful financially that I could have given her all the things she thought would make her happy. She was my mother, no matter what else, and when I needed her in my adult life she had been there for me. I was grateful for that and wished I could do more for to make her life better. Life had taken its toll on my mother and she was becoming quite frail; I didn't want anything to happen to her.

Before I knew it, David and I were back in Dublin and to our ever hectic schedule. By the end of the week Mom had been hospitalised again with acute cramps. On Friday, when I called the hospital, one of the nurses said that Mom had become very anxious and that they had moved her into a private room. We left Dublin early on Friday and spent most of the weekend with her. Something had changed. She was very frightened and told me that she thought something bad was going to happen. I told her she was being silly and that she was just a bit stressed and tired with the diverticulitis. She asked me on Sunday if I'd be able to stay longer (and I wished I could have), but reminded her that we only had two more weeks left in Dublin and we'd be back for good. I really didn't want to leave that Sunday night. Even David was asking if we could stay. My heart was heavy as we left for Dublin that evening. I was worried for Mom and I just wanted to stay with her and reassure her. I decided that I would get all my calls done by Thursday evening so that we could leave early again on Friday morning and be with Mom by lunchtime.

I got a call from the hospital on Thursday afternoon. Mom had been transferred to Tipperary General Hospital in Clonmel, after having a stroke that morning. The next forty-eight hours would be critical. I phoned my boss and made the necessary arrangements to take time off, picked David up, packed a bag and left for Clonmel. Poor Mom, she was pretty bad and my heart broke for her. She was frightened and distressed, so I stayed with her the whole time as she would only rest or sleep if I was holding her hand. The next forty-eight hours passed slowly, but without further incident. However, a scan revealed Mom had quite a severe stroke and a significant portion of her brain was no longer working. This would put a lot of pressure on her functioning brain which, we were told, would continue to weaken over time.

Marie and Alan came home from the States for a week. They both decided that it would be better to see Mom when she was alive, rather than come back for her funeral. It was a difficult situation to rationalize at the time, but the stark reality of it was that they couldn't afford to do both. Marie now lived in Montana with her husband Ray and their two children, Beth and Megan. Mom became very upset when they both walked into her room in the hospital. Seeing them both after so long shocked and frightened her and she became very agitated and confused. They both had to leave, which was upsetting for everyone.

Mom remained in a stable condition for the next few days. The matron called us into her office and told us we would have to arrange for her to go to a nursing home to continue her recovery. Alan and Marie helped and we found a lovely modern nursing home nearby. Mom was happy to leave the hospital and settled in to the nursing home within a couple of hours. She was back home again (in her own mind), and she sent me into the kitchen (her bathroom) to put the kettle on. I was relieved, thinking she'd be very upset to be in a nursing home, so I happily played along.

Alan and Marie said their goodbyes to their mother the next day before they left for the airport. They were saying goodbye for the last time, as both of them knew they would not be able to return. This journey had been a difficult one for them both. Mom knew it too and cried bitterly when they'd gone. Unfortunately, I had to return to Dublin for a few days to wrap things up and had lots to catch up on before I could start packing up our belongings. The week was hectic and after travelling down to Tipperary on Friday with a loaded car, I had to return to Dublin on Saturday to collect the rest of my belongings. Thankfully, Marian came with me and gave me a hand.

The next couple of months were busy and quite stressful. We stayed in Mom's house with David and me sharing her old bedroom, which was strange, comforting and lonely all at the same time. I found a child-minder for David and had to drop him off very early most mornings as I had such long journeys before I started work. My schedule meant that I was working in Wexford and Wicklow one week, then Cork and Kerry the next. Luckily, I had a few weeks in Limerick after that, which wasn't too bad. I had another week off when David went back to school in September. Thankfully, he settled in to his new school very well this time.

I called into Mom most evenings and sometimes she was in good form, while other times she was confused and contrary. We had a lovely night-time routine where I'd help her to have a wash and get into her pyjamas, before tucking her into bed. I'd brush her hair and put moisturiser on her face (which she loved), and then I would read to her for a while. She would call me her *true blue* and say, 'I don't know what I'd do without you Dee'. I was glad that I could be there for her and I enjoyed our time together every evening – it was nurturing for both of us.

A few weeks later, Aunty Katie and Uncle Des came to visit Mom. It was very emotional and poignant. Katie apologised, saying she should never have let her daughters get in the way of her relationship with Mom, but that they had been placed in an impossible position. She explained that she had been waiting for Sarah to come around and say that it was okay for them to see Mom again, but that had never happened. Katie said she thought that there would be more time. Mom and Katie had been like sisters for many years, and it was obvious how hurt they both were. It was awful to see them so full of regret and sadness for the lost years. And yet all was not lost: they were together again now and were reconciling the past, even if it wasn't how they imagined it. Each had been given an opportunity to say how they felt and there was forgiveness and healing – which is a lot more than some people get. The saying 'Love bears all things' was never more true. I was delighted to meet my aunt and uncle after so many years – they were the only aunt and uncle that I had ever been close to. I often thought of them when David and I were in Dublin and would have loved to have called out to see them.

Dad came to see Mom too, not long after. After hearing about the stroke from Jack, he arrived up at the hospital, begging to see her. Mom agreed to see him and of course he cried bitterly and kept apologising to her. She became agitated and told him to leave after only a few minutes, but she continued to let him call to the nursing home once she had settled in there. She regularly gave him a tirade of abuse, giving out to him and berating him constantly for hours on end. He just sat there and took it all, which surprised me; it was the first decent thing I had ever seen him do. It was amazing that Mom was finding a way of letting go of her anger and her hurt towards my father and he was finally willing to listen!

Dad was like a lost child without her and I was beginning to realise that he *was* a lost child really. Dad's childhood had been traumatic too with a raging alcoholic of a father, who used to terrorise his family with a shotgun after a night's drinking. His mother worked in the family business too and they had eleven children, which could not have been easy. Some were favoured – my father was not – and as Grandma worked, the children were mostly raised by a nanny. My dad was shown no love growing up and was most certainly abused himself by at least one Christian Brother. Nobody had taught him how to be a man, never mind a father. He was still lost in his own painful childhood. I know he caused a lot of pain and suffering to far too many people, including myself, and I could never condone or excuse his behaviour or his actions. But it was not my right to judge *him* either and I began to feel compassion for him.

Into the Light

And in this moment
I am so happy
and in this moment
I am so free.
My heart is flying
over the ocean
and the soft see breeze
Is caressing me.

And in this moment
there is light
and it is bright
and it is true.
In this moment
I am not alone
for there is me
And there is you.

(Kilkee, County Clare, 2000)

Chapter 4

Moving On

I received a call one morning from Marian's brother-in-law, Tom, who was an investor in the property market. Marian had told him that I was having trouble finding a place and asked him to keep me in mind should he find anything suitable. So when Tom came across a lovely two-bedroom, ex-council house, he thought of me. There was an asking price of one hundred thousand euro for it, but as it was a council house (and was selling privately for the first time), the buyer had to meet certain criteria to be approved by the council. Tom didn't qualify, but said that I most likely would as a single parent. Tom told me that the house was in very good condition and could be lived in with the minimum of work. He gave me the number of the estate agent and I called straight away. I was delighted as I'd been meaning to spend more time looking for my own place, but my days were so long and busy that I hadn't had the time. I made an appointment to see the house on my way home from work that day, and I was pleasantly surprised to find that I liked the small terraced house, in the quiet, little council estate adjacent to the town. Structurally, the house was sound and the windows were double-glazed. Inside, it was just like Tom said – a lick of paint would brighten it up a lot – but I could move in straight away. With prices continuing to rise, the house was great value and I went about getting approval from the council and finalising my mortgage as quickly as possible.

Christmas was coming and we decided to have Christmas dinner in Paul's house, purely because he had a reasonably sized kitchen and didn't live far from Mom's nursing home. I was focusing solely on David and Mom enjoying their Christmas day and nothing else mattered at the time. Mom still really enjoyed good food and I wanted to make her a special Christmas dinner. We stayed in Paul's on Christmas Eve and I started preparing for the big day. Christmas morning came and Santa brought David his first PlayStation and lots of other goodies. He had his sixth birthday in October and I hadn't bought him one – even though he had been hounding me all year. He decided to ask Santa for one instead and was thrilled when Santa delivered! Once I had dinner started, I went out to the nursing home, got Mom ready and brought her to Paul's. I prayed that everything would turn out well, and it did. The dinner was just perfect and Mom had a lovely time, as did David. I had spent the whole day running around and I was exhausted, but it was worth every minute of it. I wondered during the day if this was to be Mom's last Christmas with us and it was another reason to make it as special as I could.

January came and with it my mortgage approval. The county council had already approved me as a candidate for the house in late December. It would only be another few weeks before I would have the keys to my very own home. I told myself not to get too excited yet – not until I had the keys in my hand! It was a Friday when I eventually got the keys of my first home. I was overjoyed and decided to move in straight away. We spent the day shopping for bedding, kitchenware and all the usual bits and bobs. I had already picked out our beds, which were being delivered that afternoon.

Seeing Mom was not as simple now, as I was living further away from her and didn't have anyone to mind David. So I either brought David with me or called on my way home from work. I thought she might like to see our new house, so I drove her out one Sunday, but when we pulled up outside she refused to get out of the car. 'Roll down the window so I can see it,' she said, and when I did, she took one look at the house and said, 'I don't like it. Can we go for a cup of tea now?' So I brought her for afternoon tea instead – she loved her cakes and it was her favourite thing to do, though she was becoming very unsteady on her feet.

I was delighted with the house and could hardly believe that it was my very own home! The biggest outlay I had was to have a boiler and tank installed as there was only a back boiler which didn't manage to heat the radiators past warm. I bought some bedroom furniture, a sitting room suite and the basics for the kitchen. A washing machine left by the previous owners had to be replaced, as it didn't work. There was a grill and a hob, which was worked off a gas cylinder, but no oven – that would have to wait a while. I had managed to save a bit of money staying at Moms, but it was fast running out. I put in a new fireplace and painted the bedrooms and sitting room and that would have to do for a while. David picked out the colour for his room – a lovely turquoise blue – and I got him a beanbag to match. Growing up, I had never been allowed to choose anything for my bedroom – I wasn't even allowed to put up a poster on the wall – so if David had decided on cerise pink, I would have happily obliged.

My life was hectic and I was just about managing the job and home commitments. It was the amount of travelling I had to do every day that was making life difficult. I found it more challenging every day to face, and I knew that my heart wasn't in it anymore either, which made it even harder. I was no longer seeing my counsellor, Mary, either as we had come as far as we could at the time. Mary said, 'You need to get on with the business of living now Dee.' I knew she was there for me if I needed her, which was very comforting to know. I was also not seeing much of Marian either as both our lives were so busy and she was dating someone now too.

By this point, my life had already taken another turn (in a positive way) with new experiences changing my way of thinking completely. Back when I was in Dublin, I went for an Amatsu session with a wonderful practitioner by the name of Brian Peoples. Marian had given me a gift token for a session with him, as she had been to see him and was very impressed with him. Amatsu is an ancient Japanese healing art, like a holistic chiropractor with lots of other elements too. At the end of our session, Brian said that he could see me putting on a suit every day the same way that I put a smile on my face, but that my heart wasn't in my job at all and that I didn't find it fulfilling in any way. He also said he felt that I hadn't found my true vocation yet. His words rang in my ears after our session and I knew what he had said was true. I felt as if I had been given a new body, after Brian worked on me, or that my old one had been completely reprogrammed. When I went for my second session, six weeks later, Brian asked me if I had ever heard of Reiki. I said I had not, so he gave me the names of two practitioners, suggesting that I try it. One of them was a Dublin-based practitioner and the other was based in County Tipperary. I called and made an appointment with Eileen Heneghan in Tipperary, who agreed to see me on a Saturday morning (as I was still living in Dublin at the time). I found Eileen to be an extraordinary woman and my life has changed immeasurably since meeting her – a gifted, dedicated, generous, loving and compassionate woman, with wonderful insight, discernment, integrity, generosity and kindness.

The first time I went to Eileen for a Reiki session, I had no idea what was in store. We talked for a while about my life and my family and Eileen told me a little of herself and how she had worked as a nurse before becoming a Reiki practitioner. I then lay up on her plinth and within minutes I felt as if I was gently rising up through the air, travelling out of my body and out of this world. I found myself in a place that seemed both beautiful and familiar; it felt like home and I was instantly filled with peace. I became aware of these beautiful beings of light all around me and I knew I was experiencing God and Heaven in that moment. My heart became so filled with love, I thought it would burst. Tears of relief streamed down my face, as I realised for the first time in my life that I was loved; utterly, completely and unconditionally loved. There was this force of loving energy that loved me regardless of everything I had ever done, every mistake I had ever made – even every thought that had crossed my mind! I was not only loved, but I was known, intimately. I felt such joy in that moment, enveloping me like warm sunshine, but then I remembered how lonely I had been and I didn't want to go back; I didn't want to feel separate from this energy again. It was then I realised *I don't need to be separate from love, from God – that was just an illusion. I need never feel separate again. I could keep this love in my heart and the knowledge in my thoughts, always.* Eileen explained to me after our session, that everything I had suffered in the past had helped me to become more compassionate, understanding, forgiving and loving. She said that the best way to continue to heal myself would be through working with other people, that teaching what I had learned through my own life experiences would help me to continue to heal and grow. I continued to go to Eileen for healing, and also began to study Reiki with her, having already completed two of three levels of certification by the time I moved to Tipperary.

Slowly, but surely, I found that I was getting a better understanding of my life. It was like being able to step outside my little world and see the bigger picture. I had never understood why so many bad things had happened to me and couldn't see how anything positive could come from all that I had experienced. Now I could see how much I had overcome in my life and all that I had learned along the way.

I saw too that I had courage, determination and a deep desire to discover the truth – and I loved these qualities in me. I also knew that my life was moving in a different direction and I no longer wanted to be working in a job that I didn't enjoy; life was too short. I needed to be doing something that I was passionate about, that made me want to jump out of bed every morning – something that fulfilled me on a deeper level. I talked to God every day and surrendered my dreams and my worries and began to trust that I would receive help and guidance along the way. I just needed to keep my eyes and ears open!

I got a call from my boss, Tommy, late one Friday afternoon. I had just left the nursing home where Mom had been in a very agitated mood. I was tired after a long week and was feeling a little down. I didn't like the tone of Tommy's voice on the phone.

'You have to go to Galway next week,' he said. 'They're down two people and the regional manager there is shouting for you to cover the city calls. If you leave on Monday morning, you should be back Wednesday night.'

'Galway,' I echoed. 'How am I going to manage that with such short notice? What am I supposed to do with David?' I asked him.

'Look I know your circumstances, Deirdre,' he replied, 'but the job demands that you have to be flexible sometimes and it's out of my hands. Mark is insisting that you go. He's been on to the sales director about it. I'm sorry, but you'll have to sort something out.'

I felt like a mountain had just landed on my shoulders as I put my phone back in my pocket. Mark was the other regional manager and he loved to make trouble. What was I to do? Marian was on holidays with her parents and David's daytime minder, Monica, had plans too. I ended up going against all my better instincts and asking someone who I didn't really know or trust to take David for what I hoped would be only one night. Heading for Galway in the early hours of Monday morning, I was far from happy. David had not wanted me to go and was upset when I was leaving. My gut instinct was telling me not to go, but in that moment I didn't feel I had a choice.

I didn't finish my calls until about six-thirty that Monday evening. When I got back to the hotel, I ordered up some food and plugged in my computer to process all of my orders. It was three hours later before I was finished and sent my orders off from the ISDN line in my room. I kicked off my shoes and lay down on the bed. I had done a huge amount of work – nearly two days of calls in one – and I was exhausted. The plan was to get finished and home by Tuesday, instead of Wednesday. I thought of David and wondered how he was. I called the couple who were minding him and I could hear him crying in the background. I spent the next hour on the phone to David, trying to calm him down. He had really taken strange and was pleading with me to come home and I promised him I would be home the next day. I had to stay on the phone, telling him stories until he went to sleep.

I barely slept a wink that night. How could I have been so stupid? Why had I let myself be so compromised by my job? My role as a mother was more important than anything else and I had taken a chance with my son's welfare – it just wasn't good enough. What if something happened to him? I was so angry with myself and I vowed that I would never let it happen again.

Finally, the morning came and with it a phone call from David. It was only 7.00 am and he was wondering if I was on my way home yet! I knew what I was going to do next, so without hesitation I called my boss Tommy and handed in my notice. I told him that I felt compromised as a mother and that I was expected to put my job before my son, which I wasn't willing to do any more. I told him of my plans to finish the balance of the weekly calls that morning and return home that afternoon. The other calls were monthly and could be done over the phone. Tommy asked me not to be too hasty about handing in my notice and said he would meet me the following week and we could discuss it then. I thought I would never get home quick enough that day and I hugged David tighter than ever when I arrived. I told him how sorry I was and I promised him that he would never again have to stay somewhere if he didn't want to. We went for something to eat and just made the late afternoon matinee in the cinema.

When we went to see Mom that evening she was in bed with both of the safety rails pulled up. She had fallen in the bathroom the day before, bruising her face, arms and knees. She looked terrible and I had to fight back the tears. She was agitated and very unimpressed about having to stay in bed. Mom was used to being able to wander around all day because there were no stairs or steps anywhere in the building. The main door was alarmed and there were railings in all of the hallways. The nurses called her 'Sleeping Beauty' because she would often go wondering in the afternoons when the other patients were in the day room. The nurses would eventually have to look for her at teatime and usually found her asleep in someone else's room. I spoke to one of the nurses and she told me that this was Mom's third fall. 'She was lucky she didn't break her leg this time', she said. She would only be allowed up now with help and needed to use a walking frame with supervision. Of course Mom was angry with me too and wanted to know where I had been. 'It wouldn't have happened if you had been here', she said. It was another good reason to leave my job, although I might not have been able to prevent Mom's fall anyway. Much as I would have liked, I couldn't be with her all the time. I knew I would still have to work, but maybe not such long hours. I would have to trust that everything would work out. I didn't need to know how, I just knew that leaving my job was a good decision.

The following week I met Tommy as arranged in the local hotel for a coffee and an 'informal chat'. I told him that my mind was made up about leaving and that I was confident that I was making the right decision. He asked if I would work two months' notice, promising that I would not have to be away from home any night. I agreed and it was settled: I would be leaving the end of June. Marian had already asked me if I would be interested in working for her a couple of mornings a week organizing her chiropody practice, answering the phones, confirming appointments and so on. I was delighted with the offer and Marian said I could start whenever it suited me.

I was a qualified Reiki practitioner now and had also been thinking about setting up a Reiki practice at home. I couldn't help wondering if I was good enough and if I could really help others the way Eileen did. Self-doubt and worthiness issues began to plague me. I also wondered whether I would be able to support myself financially and pay my mortgage. I handed all my worries and concerns over to God and asked for guidance and support. What I felt I most needed now was a holiday for myself and David. I was feeling worn out and I had been running and racing since I started my sales training back in 2001. It was 2004 now and a lot had happened in my life since. I knew I really needed to take some time out. My boss Tommy told me the day of our meeting that I would be getting a few thousand euros of a settlement (including my shares) so I would definitely be booking a holiday of some sort, for myself and David.

I spoke to my sister Marie the following Sunday and told her how tired and worn out I felt. We had become closer since her visit home and she called often to ask about Mom.

It was so lovely when we both realised that we had so much in common and had lots to talk about. We were both reading the same kind of spiritual and self-help books by authors like Caroline Myss, Louise Hay, Deepak Chopra and Doreen Virtue. It felt like we were on the same wavelength, only five thousand miles apart! I really enjoyed our long-distance chats and wished that my sister didn't live so far away. When I explained to Marie that I was finishing up my job at the end of June she said, 'Why don't you and Dave come over here and have a well-deserved holiday with us!'

My heart skipped a beat. Was it possible? Could I afford it? I would be getting my severance payment (and mightn't be able to save money again for a while) and oh, wouldn't it be wonderful? But there was Mom.

'Look', Marie said, 'Mom will understand. You have been such a rock for her and you've had no time for yourself at all.'

'What if something happened to her when I was gone?' I argued.

'And what if you're still waiting to go on holidays in five years' time?' my sister countered. 'What will be, will be, Dee – you can't control everything. Leave it up to God like you're always telling me!'

So I did, and I booked our flights online a week later. I decided that we would stay for a month since it was so expensive to get there and I might not have the time or the money again for a while. We would leave mid-July and return mid-August. David was very excited and wanted to pack straightaway. We both deserved this break and, amazingly, Mom was much calmer about it than I thought she would be and this eased my mind too. I finished up in the job without shedding a tear. My last day's work was in Tipperary

Town and I had to drop my car back to the Toyota garage in Clonmel. Handing in the keys of my lovely Avensis was the only regret I had – I loved that car!

We left for Montana ten days later and had the time of our lives. Montana was everything I thought it would be and more. What a truly beautiful place with huge dramatic skies framed by majestic mountain ranges – most notably the famous Rocky Mountains – which were simply breathtaking. There was an abundance of forests, rivers and lakes and everything was so natural and unspoiled. I fell in love with the beauty of the place; it was Mother Nature at her very finest. Best of all was spending time with my sister and her family. David had never met any of Marie's family and I hadn't seen Ray for seventeen years. It took us all time to get to know each other better and I enjoyed every minute of it. Beth and Megan were teenagers and both were friendly, bright, beautiful, kind and very individual in their own way too. Marie's husband Ray was now a painter by trade with a great collection of brushes and baseball hats. He loved his music, his truck and his dogs. It was lovely to be a part of a family and David received lots of attention from his aunt and cousins.

One night, when Marie and I were sitting outside on the veranda, I told her about our cousin Sarah and the court case with Dad. Mom hadn't wanted anyone to tell Marie or Alan at the time, so we'd never spoken about it before. Marie was quiet before saying, 'how awful for you all.' I went on to tell her about the flashbacks and the memories that had come back to me. I even told her about what Alan had done to me. This was the first time I had spoken about anything so personal with Marie and I was a bit concerned as to how she would react. Marie was quiet for a while, before she shared her own story of childhood sexual abuse. It had never crossed my mind that something might have happened to my sister, not for a minute. I was shocked and very sad for my sister and yet it explained so much too.

We called Mom every week, but she rarely stayed on for long and usually sounded confused and unsure of who was on the phone. As we were nearing the end of our holiday, I was looking forward to seeing her again. We went shopping the day before we were set to leave and Marie bought some lovely new clothes and slippers for Mom and I bought her a warm rug. Leaving my sister and her family was heart-breaking and we all cried. Not knowing when I would see them again was the most difficult part. Marie and I promised each other that we would make more of an effort to keep in touch and to see each other more often.

As we travelled the long journey home, my mind wondered back over our wonderful holiday. It had been an amazing experience and I felt so much more relaxed, even if my heart was heavy leaving. David was like a different child: happy, carefree and with a healthy glow from all the time we spent outdoors. We had travelled to Yellowstone National Park, where we had spent two amazing days. We spent a day in Ennis Lake which was stunningly beautiful. We hired a jet-ski on the way and had hours of fun on the water. The lake was so secluded and peaceful and later, as we tucked in to a tasty picnic, I felt like the happiest person in the world. David was sitting with Marie and she was hugging him and kissing him as she chatted to him. I was chatting to Megan and Beth and I thought *this is what it feels like to be a part of a family* – it was lovely. Another day trip took us to Virginia City, an old gold-mining town which was completely deserted and had been left exactly as it was in the early 1900s. It was fascinating and felt more like the set of a Hollywood movie – we even went panning for gold. We played basketball and tennis regularly and we often went cycling up in the mountains. One of my favourite memories of all was the day we went kayaking on the Missouri River. The weather was beautiful and the scenery spectacular. I couldn't help but think that they had such a healthy lifestyle in Montana in comparison to Ireland. Most of all, though, we talked and we laughed and then we talked some more. I got to know my sister again that year and it was very special.

Three flights and five thousand miles later and we were home. Seeing Mom again was emotional for both of us and I was surprised at how relieved I felt. I could see that she was relieved too. She had lost more weight and was constantly chattering nervously to herself. I got back into our routine as quickly as I could and spent a few hours with her every afternoon or evening. I had picked up some books for Mom in the airport on the way back and Sister Stan's *Seasons of the Day* became her favourite. She was becoming more childlike every day and more fearful, needing constant reassurance. She knew she was dying and although she had great faith in God, sometimes it eluded her completely. I realised that she had worthiness issues too – she had just hidden it very well all her life. She didn't believe that she was good enough and this made her fearful about dying. I was so glad that I was in a better place myself, that I could be there for her and reassure her. Mom was fretting furiously one night when she turned and said to me, 'Dee, you'll have to help me through this; I won't be able to do it on my own.' I knew that she was talking about her passing and I said of course I would be there for her – I didn't know how, but I knew that if I was meant to be there for her, I would be.

Shortly after returning from Montana, Marie called Alan and spoke to him about what he had done to me. He, in turn, called me and apologised. He said he didn't remember much about the time, saying that he had had something of a nervous breakdown when his marriage ended. I reminded him of exactly what had happened and told him how he had hurt me deeply and how his actions made me feel, both at the time and afterwards. I told him how it had damaged me at such a delicate age in my life and how I felt ashamed, dirty and very confused about love and sex. He listened and he said he was sorry. I was careful with my answer. I didn't say it was okay as I might have done in the past, because it certainly was not okay. I thanked him for his apology and told him that I was willing to forgive him. The fact that he had listened to what I had to say and had acknowledged what had happened made it easier for me and I am grateful to him for that.

September came and David returned to school much happier and more relaxed since our holiday and all the time I was spending with him. I started working for Marian three mornings a week but this quickly became five, as there were so many things to do and the phone was constantly ringing. I had a small spare room in my house, which I turned into a healing room for Reiki and I bought a plinth and some pretty fabrics and candles. I had business cards and some brochures printed up and I put a small advert in the local paper. Some clients came to me through Marian as I left some brochures in her waiting room. I was still unsure of myself, but kept going as I needed to challenge my own worthiness issues.

This was all about self-esteem and self-belief for me and I needed to overcome these demons.

I had an appointment with Eileen, my guide and mentor, the following week. I hadn't been to see her since the start of the summer and was so looking forward to it.

My healing session was amazing as always and Eileen asked me if I had ever had an astrology reading done. I hadn't and before I left she gave me the name and number of a very gifted astrologist, Hilary. She said she felt that a personal astrology reading would be very helpful to me in understanding my past and planning for my future. That was good enough for me and when I mentioned it to Marian, she said she would like to have a reading done too. Before the week was out, we had another friend interested, so when I spoke to Hilary on the phone, we arranged that she would come down to Tipperary the following month and do the three readings in one day.

I was the first to see Hilary and didn't know what to expect. I was completely amazed by the detailed knowledge she had of my past, including trauma and abuse going back to when I was as young as three. Hilary said that I almost came undone around that age and that I had been very hurt by my father and had a difficult relationship with him and other men in the past. She told me of the constant moving house growing up, how I had become my own authority and was meeting my own emotional needs by the age of ten. I felt like the star of *This is Your Life*, as Hilary went through my life, year by year, giving accurate details of the difficulties and challenges I endured. Ultimately she said that my destiny lay in giving healing service to others, easing their pain and suffering – and said that I was yet to do deep, powerful work, helping to transform people's lives. My love of spirituality would be a driving force in my life and Hilary said I was a spiritual teacher and needed to share my spiritual values with others. I was a wise old goat after all! Through my life experiences, she said, I had learned to follow my heart and my intuition. I had also learned (through having a difficult family life), to be self-reliant and independent. I was told I had undergone a rebirth and was living my life in a new way, which I could completely relate to.

Hilary then spoke of my career and said that I would dedicate it to my mother, who in turn would guide me in my choices and decisions. She explained that my mother would be doing in the afterlife what she had not been able to do in her lifetime. There was a great deal more personal information and thankfully Hillary recorded our two hour reading, which I have got so much out of since. Hilary ended on a sadder note, as she said that my mother would not live long past her birthday in November. I don't think any experience in my life, before or since, has touched me as profoundly as that first reading with Hilary.

Mom died on the sixth of December 2004. She had just turned seventy-nine. On the previous Sunday night we had our usual routine and chat. I noticed that she was more agitated than usual and it was difficult to get her settled. I couldn't make any sense of what she was saying until I was leaving, when she clearly said, 'Don't forget me Dee.' I went back to her and kissed her on the forehead. 'Why would you say that?' I asked. 'How could I ever forget you?' I told her that I loved her again and said goodnight. I blew her a kiss as I left her room.

Not long after arriving in Marian's the following morning, after dropping David off in school, I got the dreaded call from the matron in the nursing home. She told me that Mom's heart was fading and to get there as quickly as I could. I had been expecting this moment to come and thought I was prepared for it. Yet when I hung up the phone, I began to panic; I was filled with fear for what was to come, and was overcome with sadness. It took me only fifteen minutes to get there, but it felt like forever. I prayed all the way, which helped me to calm down and compose myself. Mom had waited for me and I journeyed with her to Heaven's door, which was the greatest privilege of my life. When she let go of her life that Monday morning, I could feel her love envelop me completely. I have felt it ever since.

Marian, as usual, gave me great support and held my hand right through Mom's funeral mass. We played one of Mom's favourite songs, Debussy's 'Claire de Lune', which was very poignant, as I only found out that it was one of Mom's favourite songs in the nursing home. Aunty Katie and Uncle Des came down for the funeral. They had to endure the presence of my father, which must have been very difficult for them. It was the first time they had seen him since the court case and they had not forgiven him. Aunty Katie said she would never forgive him. I was so pleased that they were with us though and it was comforting to have their company.

It was a lonely Christmas that year. I particularly missed not having my sister around as I had been hoping that she would come home for Mom's funeral. She did consider it, but the long trip and the lonely journey home would have been too much for her to bear. Paul had booked a foreign holiday and I had no desire to spend Christmas with my father or with my brother Jack at the time. I decided to spend it in my own home with my son David; just the two of us. We were a small family – David and I – but we were a family all the same. It was the best way I could honour my mother too, and having a quiet Christmas was all I wanted that year. I bought an oven to cook the turkey in as we only had a hob in the kitchen. It was delivered the day before Christmas Eve and when I couldn't plug it in, I phoned a local electrician who arrived at the door on Christmas Eve. Gerry tried not to laugh as he explained that he would need to wire the oven, which had to have its own power box, but that he wouldn't be able to do the job until after Christmas as he didn't have the parts.

'How am I going to cook my turkey and ham?' I moaned, explaining to Gerry that I had already bought a small turkey and a half a ham. What was I to do?

'Give me one minute,' Gerry said. With that, he ran across the road and disappeared into the house opposite mine. He arrived back over a couple of minutes later with a big smile on his face. 'I was just in my mother's house and she'll cook your dinner for you,' he said.

'Are you sure?' I asked, naturally quite surprised.

'No problem at all – I'll take them over to her now if you like,' and that was that. Off Gerry went with the turkey and ham, saying he'd be in to wire up the oven the following week.

David and I spent a lovely morning together. I had put together a treasure hunt for him on Christmas Eve and he loved running around the house on Christmas morning, finding all the clues and the treasure – gold chocolate coins! We played with walkie-talkies and remote control cars and had a lovely time. Just after I lit the fire, the doorbell rang.

When I opened the door, at least fifteen members of Gerry's family were standing there, each one carrying a plate or bowl of food. 'Happy Christmas!' they said in unison. There was turkey, ham, roast and mashed potatoes, Brussels' sprouts and gravy. There was even a bowl of sherry trifle and some Christmas cake. I was almost speechless and deeply touched; what a lovely thing to do for someone they didn't even know. David came out to see who was there and I introduced us both to the family. Nellie, who was Gerry's mother, said she had heard about my mother passing and gave her condolences. They brought in all the food and wanted to know did I need anything else! They were so kind and I have never forgotten their goodness. It made our Christmas very special for me – and the food was simply gorgeous.

David got two new PlayStation games from Santa and while he was playing them that afternoon I took a little time for myself in the kitchen. I put on 'Claire de Lune', which I hadn't listened to since Mom's funeral. I opened the back door and sat down on a cushion on the back step. The sky was completely pink and everything was still and peaceful. The snow started to fall softly – as if on cue – while the music played. As the tears streamed down my face, the sun shone through the pink clouds and illuminated the falling snow. It was a beautiful, breathtaking moment and I felt surrounded by love – and by Heaven too. Even the wind chimes began to jingle softly. I could feel Mom with me and I cried and cried.

I missed Mom so much over the next few weeks. David was grieving as well. Sometimes we cried together and talked about how we were feeling. I found the nights very lonely after David went to bed. Marian had a new boyfriend and seemed very much in love. She had her first date with him the night of Mom's removal and I hadn't seen that much of her since. When Marian called in early January I was delighted. The following Friday was my birthday and Marian had booked a table at our favourite restaurant. A couple of friends of ours were going to join us for a few drinks afterwards. I thanked her and set about getting a babysitter organised.

When Friday came I was feeling very sad and emotional. It was my first birthday without my mother and I was desperately lonely for her. I hadn't expected to feel this way, but then how could I have known how I would feel! I just wanted the phone to ring and to hear Mom's voice say, 'Hi Dee, Happy Birthday love.' I cried most of the day and with a big, puffy face, I didn't feel one bit like celebrating. I called Marian and cancelled, explaining that I just wasn't able for it. I apologised and thanked her for organising the night. Marian made me promise that I would get a sitter for David and have lunch with her on Sunday instead.

Cora arrived to mind David at one o'clock and Marian and I went to the local hotel, where Marian had also arranged to meet a mutual friend, Ted, who brought along his cousin Jimmy. Ted made the introductions and we all had a lovely meal, followed by an afternoon of good conversation and plenty of brandy. I liked Jimmy straight away and felt very comfortable in his company. He had beautiful blue eyes that were shy and hard to catch a glimpse of. I really enjoyed the lunch and Marian suggested that I give my number to Jimmy before we left, as I didn't know anyone in Fethard (other than Ted, who was quite a lot older than me). Jimmy seemed happy with the suggestion, as was I.

I was walking along the riverbank in Clonmel with David the following Sunday when I got a text from Jimmy. He had been celebrating his birthday the night before and wondered what I was doing. We agreed that we would meet again in the local pub on my way home. I wondered as I drove back to Fethard if Mom was working her miracles already. She had said before she died that she would do her best to find me a decent man from 'the other side' if she could. Mom had also harped on ad nauseam, about how she would love to see me happily married. I told myself I was being silly – I had only just met Jimmy after all! We were both shy when we met again that Sunday and I wondered how Jimmy would get on with David as I introduced them to each other. It was all very relaxed and informal and we had an enjoyable couple of hours together. I could tell that David liked Jimmy straight away. Jimmy walked us home and came in for a coffee. He moved in two months later – Mom did work her magic after all! We just got on so well together and Jimmy was the most gentle natured person I had ever met.

Jimmy and I decided to have our first night away in May and Kilkee seemed like the perfect choice. I had told Jimmy about my trip there and I was keen to return. Jimmy hadn't been there before, so we were both excited to be making the trip together. As the sun was setting over the Atlantic on our first night away together, Jimmy got down on one knee and asked me to marry him.

We married on the Seventeenth of June, 2006, two months after the birth of our beautiful daughter, Sarah Elizabeth (and eighteen months after my mother's death). I asked my Uncle Des to give me away and thankfully he said he would be delighted to. Having Katie and Des there was the closest thing to having Mom there (although I knew she was with us in spirit) and it meant so much to me. I hadn't been in touch with Dad since shortly after Mom died, when he had arrived at our home one Sunday obnoxiously drunk. I didn't invite him to our wedding. Marie came from America with her family, which made it very special, and Paul came too.

The sun was shining and there wasn't a cloud to be seen in the blue sky when I arrived at the church on our wedding day. Killusty church was small and intimate and we had invited close family and friends only. 'You Raise Me Up' by Westlife was playing as I walked into the church on the arm of my Uncle Des. It was a beautiful moment and I could hardly stop the tears from flowing down my face. Des gave my arm a squeeze and patted my hand comfortingly. Tara, who I had worked with in my old life as a sales rep, was my bridesmaid. Tara and I were the first female sales reps in the company where we worked (although it seemed like a lifetime ago now), and we had become great friends. Her partner Becky came with her and had offered to do the photos as a wedding gift to us. I was delighted, since Becky was a great photographer. We had a wonderful celebration that evening and there was a very special moment when I was sitting out in the small courtyard of the hotel with Katie and Des and a few others. It was early evening and the sky was deep blue. We were talking about Mom and how she would have loved the day, when a little robin landed in front of us and proceeded to dance around the courtyard. Everyone stopped to look in amazement at the little robin, which was my mother's favourite bird (and mine too). I knew it was her, letting me know that she was with us and it was very touching and special.

I have no doubt that Jimmy is my soul mate and I am his. We have learned so much from each other and have grown stronger, both individually and together. Jimmy unfortunately grew up in an unhappy home too and has been going to counselling for the last few years. He is a wonderful, loving, kind, caring, patient human being and I love him very dearly. We have now completed our family, with the blessing of another amazing little boy, named Zach. Our son David is now ten and although he has had a lot of adjusting to do in the last few years, he is doing very well.

We have had many trials and tribulations in the last few years, but we have had many wonderful times too. I can honestly say that it has always been special and miracles continue to happen in our lives every day. I love my life and I feel very lucky and privileged to be here and to be a part of my family. There have been so many wonderful people who have helped me immeasurably along the way. I have also had the privilege of teaching others – and learning from them too – through various workshops and courses that I run on self-development, self-love, meditation and mindfulness. Jimmy and I have also attended several workshops and Reiki weekends, and I completed my Master Certificate in Reiki in 2005. I love working as a Reiki practitioner and helping other people to heal their hurts and their hearts. If there was one area of my life that I would like to improve (for me and my family) it would be to have more financial security. This is a constant work in progress, for both of us!

Before Christmas last year, I was really put to the test. Jimmy lost his job as a carpenter when Zach was only two months old. I hadn't been doing any courses since the summer and because we now had a full house, I no longer had a Reiki room as it had become Zach's bedroom. I had some regular clients who I called to, but I wasn't earning enough money to keep the household going and there was no point in advertising again until I had a place to practice. Even then, it would take me some time to build up my business again. With the building trade as slow as it was, there was no sign of Jimmy getting work again for some time. I had to consider taking a job again in sales until things improved. Within weeks, I had secured a good job and was due to start in January. My head was telling me that I had to do this, but my heart was broken. I was devastated and felt like I was taking a step backwards. What was wrong with me? I couldn't afford to be sentimental about this. We had three children to think of and mortgage repayments to make, but the battle ensued. I soon became ill with a bad chest infection, which reminded me of something Hilary had said to me (in my astrology reading), so I played the tape over again:

'You have worked in sales in the past, and you might be tempted to do so again. You mustn't, Deirdre – it's not for you and you may even become physically sick if you do not listen to your heart in this matter.'

I decided to call Eileen for advice and I told her how I was feeling. She said that I couldn't ignore my feelings anymore. I had to follow my heart no matter what the circumstances, or how impossible it seemed.

'What is your heart telling you to do?' Eileen asked me.

'To write,' I said.

And so I did...

Chapter 5

The Pot of Gold

My father came back into my life after a phone call from my brother Jack in 2009. Dad had fallen down the stairs and was in hospital with a few cuts and bruises and a broken coccyx. Jack explained that Dad had moved back in with him a couple of years after Mom died as he was struggling financially. Jack said that Dad hadn't been taking care of himself and was drinking and taking a concoction of pills at the same time. Doctors at the hospital had also raised concerns about Dad's confused state and the amount of painkillers and anti-depressants he was taking. Still, it didn't sound serious to me and I decided not to visit Dad in hospital, asking Jack to keep me updated instead.

Two weeks later Jack called again, this time in a panic. Dad had been discharged from hospital and dropped home in an ambulance. He could barely walk and Jack couldn't get him up the stairs. Without a downstairs bathroom, this was posing a serious problem and I knew that Jack wouldn't be able to deal with the situation so I stepped in to help. I was shocked when I saw Dad: the shabby, dirty clothes he was wearing and his red, blotchy complexion. He was also confused and in obvious pain. We got him a bed in a nursing home where we knew he would be properly looked after. Jack mentioned that he had been drinking and driving on a regular basis too, so we were relieved that he would be off the road, at least for the time being. They took him off all medication in the nursing home within a fortnight of being under the care of a new doctor. The matron couldn't understand why he had been taking so many pills! When Dad came out of the haze, he was not nearly as confused and disorientated as he had been. I began calling to see him in the nursing home once a week and he was pleasant and grateful too! After a while, we brought the kids to meet him – it was Sarah and Zach's first time meeting their grandfather. I was always vigilant and never let them near him or to be alone with him, not for a second. Paul began to visit him as well.

As soon as he got his strength back, I could see a change in my father. He was getting restless, agitated and fidgety. He complained regularly about the nursing home and how boring it was. He even started applying for jobs in the local paper – at seventy-nine years of age! Dad never mixed with others – he had no interest in people or their lives; he was more of a loner. He particularly disliked old people and didn't see himself as one at all! Then, one day, the matron called me to say that he was gone – a note on the table was all he had left! She was furious and initially believed that I was aware of his plans to leave. I assured her that I knew nothing and said that I was as disappointed as she obviously was by what he had done (and how he had done it). In hindsight, I should have known that this had been brewing for some time. A few weeks previously, Dad had asked me to drop his car over to the nursing home, saying that if he didn't start it up every day the battery would go flat. 'I want to just sit in my car and listen to the radio, without some old fart looking into my face,' he said. And I believed him! Dad didn't have the car taxed and his insurance was invalid too, as his doctor wouldn't give him a clean bill of health (required for his insurance) until he underwent a cataract operation which he was on a waiting-list for. I never thought for a minute that he would take off in his car like that, without discussing it with anyone. The matron of the nursing home called the police to report him as a missing person. They, in turn, called me and I told them that Dad wasn't fit to drive and that he wasn't insured. I was genuinely concerned that he would have an accident – or cause one – and that innocent people might get hurt.

Dad was stopped by the police just outside a bed and breakfast where he was staying a few days later. The policeman who stopped him called me to tell me that he was letting him go, saying he thought it only fair to give the man a chance to get his affairs sorted out. He added that Dad had no intention of returning to the nursing home and said that Dad had called it a 'mental home'! The policeman obviously felt sorry for Dad, who could obviously still turn on the charm when he wanted to. I wasn't very impressed and told the policeman that if my father was involved in an accident and hurt someone that I would hold him personally responsible!

After living in a bed and breakfast for some time, Dad was approved for a one-story council flat. Dad's social worker called me and asked if I would keep in touch with Dad if they housed him nearby. She said that it was important for Dad to have some contact with his family, now that he was old and alone. I agreed after some consideration and after filling her in on Dad's past. Before long, my father was living in a small one-bedroom bungalow around the corner from me –

I hadn't wanted him that close! He lived on there for another three years and was quite content. I sat down with him when he moved in and told him I would have nothing to do with him if he drank or if he was disrespectful to me in any way. I also gave out to him about the nursing home and said that he should have discussed leaving with the matron or with me; that it was wrong to leave the way he did. He agreed and apologised and said it wouldn't happen again.

We organised home help for Dad from Monday to Friday and I agreed to check in with him on the weekend. Unfortunately, he was still driving, as his cataract operation was a success and he'd been given the all-clear from his doctor. He drove into town most days for his lunch, parking in the disabled spot outside the pub door. He relied heavily on the two crutches that he used now.

I did Dad's shopping every week and I began to see that he was as mean with himself as he had ever been with others. The only thing he cared about was 'keeping the bank manager happy', and he lived like a pauper for it. He was just eking out an existence and not living at all. He was paranoid, too, always looking for receipts and checking his change. I don't think he trusted anyone, least of all himself. I began to see my father more objectively: he was never relaxed, never at peace and never happy. Money was the only thing that had ever smiled about. In the past, when he worked, it was always about the big order he got, or better still, the big cheque that he collected. These were the two things that made him happy, but it was always fleeting. Real happiness eluded him completely. Dad never had any friends or any kind of social life (other than poker and that was always about money too). Even his drinking was a solitary pastime; Uncle Des was the only person who'd ever gone for a drink with him. Now that I was a reasonably well-grounded and happy adult with a more positive perspective on life, I could really see how unwell my dad was and how sad his life had been.

Dad's health deteriorated and we tried in vain to get him to stop driving. We even got the local sergeant to call to him, but he wouldn't listen to anyone. In 2012, Dad had the inevitable car accident when he drove through a junction (after blacking out at the wheel) and straight into another car. Thankfully the woman driving the other car was not hurt (and was carrying no passengers), but Dad sustained quite a bad head injury, which led to him having a stroke. He has been in a nursing home since.

The next two years gave me a relationship of sorts with my father, albeit tenuous at times. Something had changed in him and I didn't believe it was simply because of the stroke: it was as if Dad had finally decided to make amends. Maybe it was because of his near-death experience after the car accident, when he held my hand and told me how sorry he was and that he wished he could change the past. He told me then that he loved me and thanked me for all that I had done for him, adding that he didn't deserve it. I never remember him telling me that he loved me, not ever. Now, in the nursing home, he said it every day. He said he couldn't change the past, but he could try to be a good father now. He also had to begin to face his own mortality, even if it frightened him. He showed an interest in my life now: concern when something was wrong, worried when I was sick. He helped us out financially on a few occasions too and even paid for me to see a specialist. He asked about the children regularly and how they were doing (though I rarely brought them to see him). Yet I began to feel very conflicted at times, with confusion and anger building up inside me. Eileen recommended that I go for counselling again and suggested the Rape Crisis Centre, as payment is by donation only and we were struggling financially at the time. I was seen by an amazing woman by the name of Frances, who has been a wonderful support to me (on and off) since. I know she is there for me if and when I need to talk. From Frances I learned that the 'dutiful daughter' was happy to call to her father, chat about the weather and make sure he had everything he needed. And then there was another part of me – a very big part of me – that was still very angry with him and didn't want to see him at all.

The counselling really helped me to see what I needed to look at around my father. I began to talk to him about the past again and how much hurt he had caused me: there was the sexual abuse (I could call it that now, even if I only had vague memories), the feelings of confusion, guilt and shame, the abandonment and emotional neglect, his drinking, the fear and loathing and what it was like growing up without any foundation or self-esteem. Dad listened and apologised every time and said he wished he could change the past and his past actions.

When I picked up the courage to confront him again about what I had seen him do in the car to Ann and how he had sexualised me as a child, he didn't deny it this time. He cried and said, 'Please don't think I'm a monster. You must think I am.' I said to him that his behaviour was monstrous and I that I would never be able to understand it or condone it; it was so wrong and incredibly damaging, confusing and hurtful. I said I would never understand how anyone could think they had the right to take away a child's innocence.

'And yet, I don't think you are a monster Dad. I know that you are sorry and that you have been trying to make amends and I'm grateful for that. I still love you and I forgive you.'

Well, my father cried like a baby and I did too. Afterwards, I felt that wonderful sense of freedom once more and it was better than ever, because the day I forgave my father was the day I stopped being a victim. Having my dad back in my life was proving to be very cathartic, even if it could also be very challenging at times. I knew that my forgiveness and my love were bringing healing to my father too. Paul began visiting Dad as well and said he quite enjoyed calling to him every week for a chat. For the first time in his life he had a father that he could talk to.

Around this time, I attended an amazing weekend workshop, working with archetypes from ancient Egypt. It was very interesting and powerful and by the end of the first day, I had a revelation of sorts. Through working with the archetypal energies I came to realise that something was blocking me from experiencing joy in my life. I didn't know what or why, but it resonated with me and I knew it was true. There were moments of joy, but it didn't come easy to me and I had also been sick a lot during the previous two years with recurring chest infections. I had even been hospitalised with pneumonia in January that same year, so my body was telling me something too.

There was also the fact that Jimmy and I seemed to be constantly struggling financially – caught up in the old patterns of lack and limitation that we had both grown up with. I asked God and the Angels, in bed that night, to reveal to me in my dreams whatever was blocking me from feeling joy. I woke up in the early hours of the morning, sobbing hysterically, as I pleaded with Ann's mom Helen to forgive me. In my dream, I was a child again and our family was helping Sophie and Ann's family to move house. They had all these big brown boxes that wouldn't fit in the removal truck. I told them that they could keep their boxes in our house! When I found myself alone with Helen in the dream, I began to cry and tell her how sorry I was, that I had seen what my dad had done to Ann and I hadn't done anything to stop him; I hadn't protected her. The grief and pain that I felt was so intense that it woke me and Jimmy held me as I sobbed into my pillow. I knew enough about psychology to understand the dream and the symbolism in it – I was obviously still carrying feelings of enormous guilt and shame. Sharing my dream with the group the following day, I was overcome with the feelings of guilt and shame once more.

The following week I went over the whole experience in counselling. Frances said that I'd obviously been holding on to this guilt around Ann and her mom for a long time and asked, 'what do you need to do, to let go of this guilt now Dee?'

Without pausing I answered, 'I need to apologise to Helen. I want to go and see her and tell her I'm sorry. I need to do this and I feel very strongly about it.' I was even surprised, by my answer and I knew it was coming from the child inside me who was obviously very determined. We teased it out a bit and I decided to write to her first.

A month later and I was sitting on a train, making my way to Skerries. Helen had agreed to meet me in a local coffee shop for a chat and I was nervous and excited all at once. I had booked a bed and breakfast near the village and would return home the following day. The plan was to spend some time by the sea, have a meander around the places where I grew up and just have a bit of time to myself. My mission was to make peace with my past and I was hoping that this trip would help in that process.

Helen knew that there was something that I wanted to talk to her about, but I hadn't been more specific. I wondered if she had an idea, as I ordered a coffee and sat at a quiet corner table. Recognising Helen the moment I saw her (she hadn't changed much at all in the thirty years since I'd seen her last!), I stood up to give her a warm hug. After we had exchanged a few pleasantries and Helen was sipping her tea, I showed her a picture I had of my dad with myself, Sophie and Ann on our communion day. She became instantly uncomfortable and I knew straight away that she knew. I told her about Ann and about the guilt that I felt and how terribly sorry I was.

Once I had said the words, 'I am so sorry', it was as if a huge weight was lifted off my shoulders. Helen was so understanding and kind and said that I wasn't to blame at all. I asked how Ann was, as I often worried about her, especially as she was so quiet and sensitive. Helen said that she was doing great: Ann was happily married with a lovely family and not living too far from Skerries. I wasn't expecting to hear what Helen had to say next:

'You know that he abused Sophie too?'

'What?' I replied, as my stomach rose up into my mouth. 'No,' I almost whispered, 'not Sophie too?' I could hear a voice inside me say *I thought I had protected her*. Did the child inside me know more than I did? It would seem so.

'Yes, I'm afraid so,' Helen said. 'She's doing great considering everything and her attitude is so positive. Sophie has bipolar disorder and, well, she's been through a really tough time.'

Helen went on to explain that it all came to light when Ann and Sophie were young adults. Ann remembered first and then Sophie started having problems with her first boyfriend and it went from there. I asked her if they had ever thought about bringing charges against my dad. Helen said that they had sat down as a family and discussed it, but decided that it would be better for everyone to leave it in the past and get on with their lives. I told her about my cousins, Ellie and Sarah, and how Sarah's case had gone, with Dad not serving one night in jail even though he was found guilty. Helen seemed relieved and I could see that their decision not to take things further had weighed heavy on her mind. She asked me if I had ever thought about prosecuting my father. I explained that although I had done a lot of counselling, my memories were still too vague and that I wished I could remember exactly what had happened. She asked about Mom then, as they had been quite friendly back when they were neighbours, and she was sad to hear of her death.

We talked about Sophie some more and Helen told me that she was married and living in Carlow. She had no children. I expressed an interest in meeting her again and Helen said that maybe Sophie would like to meet me too. Not wanting to cause any upset to her, I explained to her about my cousins being unable to have any contact with anyone in my family and assured her that I would understand completely if Sophie would rather not meet with me. Helen said that the family were very protective of her naturally and said that she would give the matter some thought and let me know. I thanked her for taking the time to meet with me, especially when I was bringing up the painful past. I added that I was very grateful to her and that having the opportunity to talk had allowed me to let go of the guilt that I had been carrying for years. She asked only that I never mention it to her again and I promised that I never would. She asked also that if I did meet Sophie that I was not to mention anything of my father or ask her about the past at all. I agreed, but really wasn't too hopeful of ever meeting my old friend again.

I went for a long walk by the sea as I gathered my thoughts and my feelings. There was no doubt that I felt hugely relieved of the burden of guilt that I had been carrying – that was the reason I had made the trip in the first place. And it had all gone so well until Helen told me about Sophie having been abused too. Why had it never crossed my mind before? It was the truth and finding out the truth usually made me feel so much better. So why did I feel such sadness and pain?

I headed for the sea, where I knew I would find solace. I always found the sea soothing and relaxing and after walking for a while I sat on a rock for hours, letting my thoughts come and go, like the waves. The weather was lovely for autumn, but it became cooler as the afternoon progressed, so I walked back to the town, had something to eat and retired to my bed and breakfast. I was tired after my early start and I hadn't slept well the night before either. I wondered how many more there had been, how many more innocent children? I remembered finding random toys in Dad's car and I felt my chest tighten and panic well up inside me. And Sophie, if ever there was an angel born on this planet, it was her. With her dimples, her golden blond curls and her sweet, infectious giggle! I remembered how kind she was and how she cared deeply about every living thing. How could he? It was inconceivable to me.

I was glad I had some time to myself to process all that was going on in my mind. When I woke the following morning, I could feel my chest wheezing once again. There was no doubt in my mind that whatever was going on with me emotionally was effecting me physically. The lungs represent grief in Chinese medicine — and I was surely grieving.

When I returned to home (and had recovered from my chest infection), I sent Helen a letter thanking her again, along with a copy of the 'Serenity Prayer', which I picked up in a local shop, and two angel cards for Sophie and Ann. The following week, I received a text from Sophie saying that she would love to meet me! Her message was so warm and friendly, it took a while to sink in. When it did, I was delighted and excited. We arranged to meet in Kilkenny the following week. Forty years after we first became acquainted in my front garden I was going to meet the first friend I ever had and one of the sweetest people I had ever known. My father had torn us apart and was, inadvertently, bringing us back together again.

Driving up to meet Sophie, I really believed that this would be the happy ending I was waiting for. It might also be the perfect ending for this book (which I had been working on for over three years at this time). I didn't recognise Sophie when I first saw her, but when she smiled over at me and revealed her lovely dimples I knew it was her. We hugged and I cried a little too. However, I soon realised that this was not going to be the reunion that I had hoped for. Sophie was obviously on a lot of medication and I was taken aback – I just wasn't prepared. I had met people with bipolar before, through my work with the mental health services, and I wouldn't have known that they had any mental impairment until they told me. The demons that Sophie had obviously been fighting had left their mark and I could see that she was still fighting a daily battle. We spoke about the past, about school and Sophie asked me all about my life. She brought a photo album with some beautiful pictures of herself growing up, her college days and her early years working as a teacher. There were some pictures of us in it too – one was of Sophie's seventh birthday party. She told me that her college days were the happiest days of her life. I got the sense that Sophie thought that the best of her life was over. When we got up to go for a bit of a walkabout, I noticed she had a bad limp; I remembered what Mary had said, so I didn't ask about it. We parted company shortly after with a very big hug, and as I walked back to my car I tried to hold back the tears. What had happened to Sophie? The pictures that she had showed me were of a beautiful, smiling, confident young woman – just as I had imagined her to be. Where had she gone? Was my father responsible for this? How had I escaped mental illness and Sophie had not? Why was life so unfair? Why couldn't I have my happy ending?

I felt the most enormous sadness and grief as I drove home that day and had to stop the car three or four times, I was crying so much. Jimmy was waiting for me when I got home and just held me as I sobbed. Another chest infection ensued and I had to dig deep to keep the despair (which was closing in on me) at bay. I went to see Dad as soon as I could face him and told him everything, calmly and with as much compassion as I could manage. Why should he be spared from the truth, I thought, he needs to hear this. He was quiet for quite some time before he described himself as a monster once more, and said that if there was a hell that he was sure to be going there. I don't believe in hell – not as a place anyway. I believe that we have to live with our actions and their consequences. What we don't face in this lifetime, I'm sure we have to face in the next (and with the full awareness of what we have done and the hurt that we might have caused). That is surely hell enough for some! I left him sitting with himself and his thoughts that day and couldn't bring myself to visit with him for a while after. I had to find a way through this myself first.

Marie phoned me shortly after my trip to Dublin. I knew she was concerned about my constant chest infections and all the steroids I had been taking, so when I told her about meeting Helen and Sophie she said, 'don't you think it's time you stopped digging now Dee and let go of the past?' I knew she was right and I also felt that I had done all that I could do. I could do no more now, except move on with my life. I had always wanted to remember exactly what happened with Dad, other than hearing his voice change and feeling him touch me as he bumped me up and down on his lap. Maybe it wasn't to be; maybe it was better that I didn't remember. But then I wondered: what if I remembered out of the blue one day and I wasn't able to cope? What if my mental health became affected? What then? I had always searched for the truth and I would always welcome the truth – I just had to stop digging for it. I also had to accept that life didn't always have fairytale endings. There was the good, the bad and the ugly; life had it all and maybe it was fitting that my story was real and that everything didn't work out perfectly.

Sophie decided shortly after we met in Kilkenny that it would be best if we did not stay in touch. She said that our decision to meet had become an issue with some of her family and she had to respect their wishes. I said that I understood and we wished each other the very best for the future. I remember Sophie and her family every day in my prayers and I hope they are well and happy. I admire the courage and determination that she has and I am so grateful to have had the opportunity to meet with her and her mother. Maybe it was best to leave it in the past now. Meeting my childhood friend had been special and the best way I could honour our friendship (and my memory of her) was to live my life and live it to the fullest, be the best that I could be and help as many people along the way as I could.

Dad was admitted to hospital in early December 2014 with pneumonia. He was very ill and his liver and kidneys were failing. Doctors told us that there was a ninety per cent chance that he wouldn't make it. I spent a lot of time with him then – he could hardly breathe at times and he was very frightened. When he was able to talk it was of his father and family, who he'd never spoken about before. Dad's fear was palpable and he fought really hard to stay alive. No matter how much I reassured him, he just wouldn't let go. Gradually, and against all odds, he started to improve and was discharged back to the nursing home a week later. I invited him for Christmas dinner and Paul agreed to collect him and bring him to our house, as he was coming for dinner too.

Christmas came around fast and we had a lovely morning with the kids before Paul arrived with Dad. There was something different about my father, but I couldn't put my finger on it straight away. I sat him beside me at the table and away from the children as always. While we were eating dessert (thankfully, the kids had finished theirs and were watching a film in the sitting room), I rubbed my hip absentmindedly, as it was a bit stiff and sore. Dad became very concerned and asked me what was wrong. He reached out toward me and started talking about rubbing it with his fingers. He held out his three fingers together: 'You'll love it,' he said. 'It'll make it all better. You'll love it, love it, love it,' he almost whispered. His voice was soft and caring, but he didn't normally speak like this and I was beginning to feel quite spooked. There was definitely something intimate about the way he spoke – something sexual even – and I could feel the hairs on the back of my neck stand up. Dad was looking out the window now, whispering to himself. I heard the words 'suck it.' *He doesn't know what he's saying,* I thought to myself. *He's in a world of his own.* I heard him say the words again: 'come on, suck it.' *He's not talking to me,* I assured myself. *He couldn't be talking to me.* The next words I heard were 'Deedee... Suck it Deedee. Suck the big one Deedee.' I will never forget those words.

My heart nearly jumped out of my chest as I leapt from the chair and practically ran from the room. I don't remember getting from the kitchen to my bedroom, so I must have momentarily blanked out. I just remember sitting at my dressing table, shaking from head to toe. *I don't want to Daddy. Daddy don't; please Daddy don't,* I heard myself say. I couldn't stop the memories now – the horror of it all was overwhelming. I had to get him out of my home. I gathered myself after about ten minutes and went back down to the kitchen, where I made a beeline for Paul and asked him to take Dad home. Paul didn't ask any questions, so I knew he had an idea that something was amiss and didn't hesitate in getting Dad out of there. I went around in a daze for the next week. Sarah and Zach woke up with the chicken pox on Saint Stephen's Day and they were both very sick for the week. Thankfully, they didn't really notice that their mom wasn't herself. I ran a bath one night after the kids were settled in bed and I let the tears finally came as I lay in the water. I went to the darkest place inside me that night and there are no words to describe the pain – the hurt and the sorrow that I felt that night. It eventually passed and other than feeling incredibly tired, I felt at peace with myself.

What stunned me the most (but was also the most helpful revelation) was that my father only ever behaved lovingly towards me when he was being sexual, and this had really confused me as a child. It had also confused me in my adult relationships and now I understood why. Also, there was a part of me (regardless of everything I had ever felt, and everything I had ever seen my dad do), that said, 'maybe he didn't touch me. Maybe I imagined it. Maybe it was no big deal'. I had always tried to minimise everything, which is not unusual for victims of sexual abuse, but it can be very unhelpful. Finally, I knew for certain what had happened – and although there was huge pain and loss in that truth – it was enormously healing. Simultaneously, I began to feel much happier and I found myself laughing a lot more. I felt somehow lighter! And I felt joyful! My father had given me the best gift of all: the truth, and on Christmas day too!

I went to see my father a couple of weeks later and explained to him how his behaviour had affected me; that what he said to me had been very upsetting and traumatic. 'You are my father and I am your daughter,' I said. 'If this happens again I won't be able to see you anymore.' He said he was sorry, but didn't seem to know what I was talking about. Since Christmas, I am naturally less comfortable around him and have been going to see him only when I feel like it – usually every two to three weeks. I don't stay long any more either. We talk about God sometimes and about death as I know how afraid he is. I've told him that I believe that there is only love waiting for him when he dies and I wish he would believe me, but I know he is full of doubt and fear. His mental health has continued to deteriorate since and there are days now when he's living a completely different reality – he's in a music band or he's starting a new business or in the process of buying a new house. I play along with whatever he thinks his current reality is but there is no real communication anymore. I don't believe he's there anymore, not really.

I know it may sound strange, and may be difficult to understand, but he is still my father and yes, I do love him and I forgive him. It has taken me a very long time, but I have forgiven him. I think we have both let each other go in a lot of ways. He has been my biggest teacher and maybe I have been one of his. I feel that our work is done in this lifetime, if that makes any sense? What my father has done to others is not mine to forgive. I just hope that his other victims have found forgiveness and peace for themselves too.

My father has missed out on so much in his life and I feel sorry for his suffering and the suffering he has caused others. As long as I have known him, he has never been at peace and that is so sad for him. I have only a few pleasant memories of my father – snapshots of moments of kindness – moments that mattered to me. When I was a child and was sick and bed-ridden, my father would always bring home a bottle of

Lucozade (the original one with the golden wrapper) and a magazine like 'Bunty' or whatever I was into at that time. I'm sure it was only a few times but I remember wishing that I would get sick more often. There have also been the last couple of years (before Christmas) when I saw that Dad was genuinely concerned about me, when I was having health problems and when we were having some financial problems too. He was supportive, caring and generous during this time and for the first time in my life he was there for me and genuinely wanted to help me any way he could. I will always have those precious times no matter what else happened and nobody can take them away from me. For all he did, I know that he loves me in his own way. This is still hard to reconcile with the deviant paedophile with the twisted and toxic mind, who has also been my father in this life of mine. What has always hurt the most, and continues to hurt, is my father's absence from my life. I still cry about this sometimes and I realise that I've been missing him my whole life.

We hear from my Aunt Katie and Uncle David from time to time. They came down to Tipperary this summer and we spent a day together. It was lovely to see them, but what made this year so special was that we didn't talk about the past, or about Dad at all. They are restricted in the contact they can have with us on account of how their daughters still feel. They also find it difficult to accept or understand the contact I now have with my father, but that is understandable. The relationships that I have with my siblings is challenging at times – Marie and I do our best to keep in touch (not easy being so far away), Paul and Jack have a very different outlook to me and this can be challenging at times (I'm sure for them too!). We may not be close, but I know that we all love each other and we must continue to make an effort in each other's lives.

I think of my mother often and know that she is still a part of our lives. Before our daughter Sarah was born I had a recurring dream, where I was standing at our front door, watching Mom walk towards our house. She was smiling and looked very happy as she drew nearer. Her lower body was hidden by a wall, but when she came into full view I could see that she was holding the hand of a little girl with blond hair. I could see the girl's face clearly. It is our lovely little girl, Sarah. Mom was letting me know that she was with Sarah on her journey to us. Sarah ended up being an emergency section, but I knew when I was being rushed down to surgery, and heard the doctor saying 'we've got ten minutes,' that Mom was with us and I knew everything would be okay.

There have been times, since her death, when I have felt enormous anger and hurt towards her too. I was doing some regression work with a kinesiologist some time ago and I was back in my mother's kitchen, at about the age of six. I asked my mother a question and her answer was, 'I'm busy.' In that moment I remembered that she said 'I'm busy' all the time and it made me feel very angry. As I grew up, my mother regularly hijacked my life, emotionally blackmailed me and expected me to put her needs before mine. And yet, she was there for me as an adult and was always supportive and loving. She did her best and I forgive her faults and failings with all my heart. She didn't have an easy life and something she shared with me in later life helped me to understand her much better. Her greatest crime was giving up on herself, but at least now I understood why. I know my mother watches over all of us and is doing a great job.

The most important realisation for me is this: I am the happy ending. ME! I made it. I survived my awful childhood and I even survived remembering my awful childhood. I survived the very rocky road of growing up on my own. I survived promiscuity and sleeping with someone who was HIV positive. I survived being raped. I'm not only alive, but I'm happy and healthy and I give thanks every morning for my life, for my family – for all that I have and for all that I am.

In my early years of counselling I treated my past and my pain like a broken leg – once it was mended, everything would be okay again and I would be 'normal.' It took me a long time to realise that what happened to me was so much bigger than a broken leg and that it would affect me for the rest of my life in one way or another. There are times that I am plagued by self-doubt. I struggle with needing approval from others sometimes and I find it hard to trust my own instincts, but I am learning and growing every day and, thankfully, I don't have to be perfect. My past doesn't have to define me, but it is a part of me and that's okay. I wouldn't swap the person I am now for anyone else. I'm proud of who I am, who I have become, and I'd like to share with you in the next section what I have learned along the way.

Lift up the self by the Self
And don't let the Self droop down,
For the Self is the self's only friend,
And the self is the Self's only foe.

– From the *Bhagavad Gita*

Part 2

Lessons Learned

Chapter 6

Avoiding Pain and Finding Courage

Courage: the most important of all the virtues
because without courage, you can't practice any
other virtue consistently. – Maya Angelou

I have met a lot of people who have had painful childhoods, or at least some degree of pain stemming from their family situation. Many find themselves dealing with, or trying to understand, this pain as adults. For some, it is a strict, domineering, demanding father; for others it may be a mother who was emotionally detached and incapable of affection. Sometimes, the pain comes from a parent being absent or maybe from someone knowing that they were given up for adoption by their mother. There are lots of reasons and some of us have had it worse than others, but pain is pain, whether we have a lot of it or a little, and it can cause some very destructive patterns in our lives if we don't deal with it. There is no avoiding pain if we want to be free of it; we can't go around it, under it, over it or hang around waiting for it to go away, because it won't. We must go through it and open up to it if we are to let it go.

For some reason, though, we have become afraid of our feelings and we have become very good at finding ways to avoid our emotions. We busy our minds constantly. We eat too much or drink too much. We work too hard. We fixate on others and their needs. In other words, we lose balance in our lives. We forget the value of being connected to ourselves and to enjoying the stillness within us. We can become lost as we try to avoid our feelings, because we have to stop listening to ourselves. The worst thing about avoiding our feelings is that we continue to carry them around inside us until we are willing to face them. What a heavy burden they can be, and how can we feel peace in our lives with all of these emotions clambering to get out!

I believe that the emotions that came up for me, as I worked through my pain, are the same for most people and I hope that my story will help anyone who has experienced any kind of pain growing up. You don't have to have been abused sexually or physically to have feelings of hurt, sadness, confusion, guilt or anger. Whatever feelings you have are valid and real because they are yours and it is okay to have them. If you want to be free and heal the hurts, it is vital that you find ways to express your feelings. There have been times when I feared becoming overwhelmed by the old bottled-up feelings and this is perfectly natural too. The feelings were overwhelming at the time so there's bound to be some residual fear around taking off the lid. I don't think we give ourselves enough credit though. Whatever we felt and whatever happened, we have already survived and it's only the memory and/or the feelings associated with it that we have to release. We don't have to experience what happened all over again. We just have to open up the door and release it.

My understanding of suppression is that it happens when our minds bury the event, trauma or abuse to protect us. This survival technique or coping mechanism stops us from becoming overwhelmed by what happened to us. The memory is buried in the subconscious mind and it is often later in life that something triggers the memory or a feeling associated with it. Sometimes spontaneously, or more often over a period of time, the whole event or memory will come to the surface. Other times it can be that another family member will remember first, or a memory can be triggered by a similar story in the news. Also, our first sexual encounter can bring with it feelings of confusion and shame. The birth of a child can also trigger old memories or feelings from our subconscious.

In my case, it was my cousins' conversation with me about their abuse by my father that began the flashbacks for me. Another common trigger is the end of a relationship, which can often bring up painful abandonment issues from childhood. With my sister Marie, she began to have flashbacks and nightmares after the birth of her daughter. Speaking up and talking about abuse not only starts the healing process for the victim, but it also allows others, who may not have been previously aware of having been abused, the opportunity to heal. I am grateful to my cousin Sarah for opening the door in my mind for me. Unfortunately, for some, the memories never come to the surface as they are buried so deeply, but the process of healing can still happen if an individual is willing to look at destructive life patterns or pervasive feelings of guilt, shame, anger and unworthiness in their lives.

When we do start to remember past hurts or traumas that have been suppressed, it is very important that counselling is sought. There are many stages of emotions that a person goes through and although I address them in the following chapters, it is necessary that we all take our own unique healing journey and explore our own emotional issues. We are then free to get on with our lives, without all the baggage that abuse and trauma bring. There is no doubt that looking at our pain, our deep hurts, takes courage, but opening up to it is the only way to heal it and ultimately be free of it. I have seen so many people choosing to run away from their pain and from their past, but they are never free of it and are never at peace with themselves. Once they start running, they have to keep denying themselves and their feelings and this causes so much more pain in the long run. We are all so much stronger than we give ourselves credit for and have more courage than we know ... and as the prayer goes:

> *God grant me the serenity to accept the things I*
> *cannot change, the courage to change the things I*
> *can and the wisdom to know the difference.*

Fear only exists in our imagination, and it's important that we learn to face the fear of our emotions rather than let them paralyze or debilitate us. It is fear that can keep us stuck in really unhappy relationships (with ourselves and others), in destructive patterns of behaviour, unfulfilling jobs and so on. We can be afraid of change and afraid of the unknown to such a degree that we would prefer to stay with what we know (even if we're unhappy and unfulfilled), rather than face change or uncertainty. Ironically, change will happen anyway, regardless of whether we have an aversion to it or not.

Decide not to be afraid of change, to see it instead as a positive force in your life. Making decisions and creating changes in our lives is positive and empowering. The future is uncertain and we have no control over it anyway, so we may as well hold a positive outlook about it, without dwelling on it either! We can only live in the present and we need to focus on being happy and fulfilled and not be afraid to make decisions that support our well-being. We need to take chances, to jump into the unknown, to get out of our comfort zone and treat life as an adventure!

Chapter 7

Denial, Addiction and the Cycle of Abuse

Healing from childhood abuse within the family is not easy, but it is possible. My childhood was very dysfunctional as my father was an alcoholic as well as a paedophile, and my parents were unhappily married. My mother was co-dependent, which made separating from her husband difficult. It was something she was not able to do until late in her life and she was never capable of living on her own. I believe that both my parents had their own demons that played out in their lives (and in ours). My grandfather (on my father's side) was an alcoholic and often terrorized the family late at night with a shotgun! My mother never even spoke of her family – that said a lot in itself.

I would love to know how to stop the sexual abuse of children and I believe it begins with openness and understanding. Statistically, most abusers were themselves abused as children and there the cycle begins. I believe that a lot of abusers are stuck in denial and have never come to terms with their own abuse. They may act out in a misguided attempt to regain their own lost power. It is necessary that child sexual abuse is regarded as a criminal offence and it needs to be taken very seriously – the protection of children must be a societal priority. I do believe, however, that paedophiles, generally speaking, are victims too and need to be given extensive psychotherapy, particularly if they are to be released back into society again.

But anyone who is in a state of denial, through any form of compulsion or addiction, cannot begin to heal. So how and what are we denying? Well, denial takes on many guises: it didn't happen, it was normal, nobody is perfect, it could have been worse (or others have had it worse) and so on. We make comparisons, we do damage limitation, we minimise; we do whatever we can to deny what happened. So, what are we really denying? Our feelings, ourselves, our truth.

When we acknowledge that something happened, we have to acknowledge our feelings about it. The same is true for a compulsion or addiction: we have to do something about it. If we acknowledge that it is a problem we then have to face it. Denial keeps us trapped, and of course fear is the usual motivating force behind denial. The other thing to remember about addiction is that it changes the way we think and acts like a parasite in our brain. Neuroscience has come very far in understanding how the brain functions and we now know that addiction changes the brain, first by subverting the way it registers pleasure and then by corrupting other normal drives such as learning and motivation. It can be hard to change your reality if that reality is distorted!

A lot of addictions are faced and dealt with over time. Most addicts will face their addictions at some stage in their lives: after marital separation, loss of a job, lack of money or for health reasons. Sometimes their families have put them under severe pressure to face up to their problem and this can eventually also bring about acceptance. There are exceptions too, of course – those who die from their addiction or those who manage to keep some degree of control and management in their lives. Addicts have choices. They can go to their doctor who will support a detox treatment, and there are numerous treatment centres and clinics all over the country which treat alcoholism, drug addiction and gambling. There are also the less obvious addictions like compulsive eating, anorexia, bulimia, sex, lying, cheating, unhealthy and damaging relationships and so on. People can even become addicted to having to control everything and everyone in their lives. Here's where psychotherapy can help. One thing I do know about addiction or compulsion is this: a person may become sober, stop gambling or over-eating or whatever they have become compulsive about, but if they don't deal with what is causing them pain (and what led to their addiction in the first place), they will never heal and they will more be more likely to relapse or find another addiction.

With regard to child abuse, it is lamentable considering that one in four people in Ireland have been victims of child abuse that there is nowhere (other than a very small prison in Dublin, known as Arbour Hill), for the treatment of their perpetrators, as far as I am aware. When a child is sexually abused, their power is taken away from them. Some adult survivors turn to the same behaviour in a misguided attempt to regain their power, while others continue to give their power (and themselves) away as adults, as I did. I'm sure it must be similar with children who were physically abused. As a society, we are allowing denial to continue through secrecy and an unwillingness to talk about child sexual abuse and the people who abuse children in our families and communities. This enables abusers to continue abusing and to live in a state of denial. This needs to change and we need to stop burying these issues under the carpet, because these days that carpet is also a growing underworld of child pornography, played out on the internet, where vulnerable children around the world are horrifically abused while being filmed and these shocking images being shared with other paedophiles.

So why do children who were sexually abused often engage in abusive relationships in their adult lives? This may be as a victim, an abuser or (as is often the case) as both. Maureen Canning, herself a child abuse survivor, recovered sex addict and relationship therapist, explains the many reasons in her book, *Lust, Anger, Love: Understanding Sexual Addiction and the Road to Healthy Intimacy*. Her top ten reasons sexually abused children grow up to have abusive relationships in adulthood include:

(1) It feels familiar. If the connection between abuse and "love" is made early in life, the feelings of shame and anger, which naturally happen as a consequence of the abuse, are interpreted as feelings of love and passion. People who have been abused may not realize other ways of feeling in relationships are possible. They believe they are feeling love for their abuser, so when they are later abused in an intimate relationship, they perceive the familiar feelings of shame and anger as love and passion.

(2) It is an attempt to heal. By becoming an abuser, a victim of childhood sexual abuse can try to undo the abuse by taking the opposite, seemingly more powerful, position.

By engaging in a relationship with another abuser, they can try to relive the relationship with their original abuser in the hope that they can get it right this time.

(3) They feel inadequate. People who were abused as children may believe, on some level, that they are not good enough to deserve a genuinely caring relationship. They feel in a one-down position to others, making it hard to accept real love. They may have even been convinced by their abuser that they deserved the abuse.

(4) They feel grandiose. People who were abused may also feel, on some level, that they are better than others, and have a hard time respecting other people as equals. They feel in a one-up position to others, making it hard to enter a mutually loving, respectful relationship. They may even feel one-down to some people, and one-up to others, engaging in abusive relationships at the same time they are being abused by others.

(5) It is a search for power and control. By becoming an abuser, someone who has been abused can play the role of the more powerful person in the relationship in an attempt to overcome the powerlessness they felt when they were being abused.

(6) They may be sexually aroused by abusive behaviour. In some cases, if early sexual experiences involved abuse, they may become sexually aroused by abusive behaviour. This does not mean they want or wanted to be abused, or that they genuinely enjoy abuse, and not all victims of abuse experience this.

(7) They feel very angry. People who have been abused carry a lot of anger about what happened to them, and abuse can be a way to express that anger.

(8) They may try to hurt others before being hurt. If abuse and hurt feels inevitable, people who have been abused may view sexual relationships as predatory and try to 'kill before being killed'.

(9) They are searching for intensity. When children are traumatized through sexual abuse, they may associate or confuse intensity with pleasure. They may be attracted to abusive individuals and high-risk activities in order to feel pleasure, as they need the rush of danger in order to feel aroused or to experience orgasm.

(10) Living a fantasy feels safer than reality. Because abuse is so painful, people who have been abused may cope by retreating into a fantasy world. This may include idealizing others to the point where abusive partners are seen as wonderful, or others are abused as a result of the overwhelming disappointment felt when they cannot live up to the fantasy.

We need to be brave and to face the shadow-side of human nature with compassion and understanding and without judgement. It is usually a lack of love and confusion about what love is that leads to these behaviours; it is surely love and understanding that is needed to heal them.

Chapter 8

The Armour that Is Anger

'You know, you can take off your amour now, Dee,' my counsellor Mary said to me one day, 'the war is over.'

I was a bit confused and unsure what she meant. I had been seeing Mary for about six months at this point and felt that I was making good progress.

'There is no need to fight anymore or be so defensive,' she continued, 'there's nobody attacking you. There is no danger in any way; you're safe now.'

I sat back in my chair and thought about what she had just said. Her words really resonated with me and it took a few minutes to sink in; I had been angry for so long and I didn't know how else to behave. I had felt protected by my wall of anger in the past and it had kept me safe, but I was getting tired of it and it was a lonely place to be. The time had come and I knew Mary was right – her timing was impeccable as always. I was uncertain of how I would feel if I let it go, yet I knew that I had to if I was to move forward. I couldn't reach out to other people for friendship or support, and woke up feeling grumpy (angry) every morning, which I carried with me every day. It affected my relationship with my son, David, as I had very little patience with him and was often distracted or irritable. Having fun in my everyday life was difficult and I could see that what had been familiar and safe was no longer serving me well. I also knew that I needed to face what lay underneath the anger.

Embracing change is never easy as it is a step into unknown territory. It begins with knowing and accepting that change is good, and then learning to embrace change as if it were a good friend, always bringing us forward in our lives. I made a conscious decision in that moment to let the anger go. A wave of relief came over me as I felt as if something had physically lifted off me. My 'suit of anger' was hot and heavy and had been restricting me in many ways. I could not continue to grow through anger and was glad that my war was finally over. My eyes filled up with tears.

'How are you feeling now, Dee?' Mary asked.

'Very sad,' I said, after a moment.

'It's okay, just let it come,' she said, and I did.

I was incredibly sad, but also relieved that I was finally acknowledging the sadness that I had always known was there. I didn't feel overwhelmed by it even though I knew there was a huge amount of sadness inside me. I knew now that I could work through this sadness and let it go the same way that I had with my anger. I didn't have to be a prisoner of my emotions any more. I left my counsellor that day feeling lighter and freer than I had ever felt before. I also felt joy within my sadness because I felt alive again and more connected to myself. I was moving forward, unrestricted, and I was grateful for it.

Anger is a very necessary part of the healing process. Each one of us has a right to feel anger and it is important that we learn to express it in appropriate and respectful ways. This can be easy enough to do with everyday anger by simply stating that we are feeling angry and explaining why. Being able to say, 'I am feeling angry with you', or 'I feel angry about whatever', is a wonderful and positive thing. It empowers us and diminishes the anger straight away.

A lot of us were not brought up to express anger so openly: anger was often disapproved of and we wrongly learned that we didn't have a right to be angry. If we did express anger, we were punished for it, so we learned to bottle it up which created many unhealthy ways of expression. There are so many words that we use to describe anger: *pissed off, grumpy, irritable, moody, irate, annoyed, in bad form, in a mood, bitchy, argumentative* and so on. We even blame others by saying '*they are annoying me, doing my head in...*' etc. We don't want to own our anger so we try to distance ourselves from it. When we take responsibility for our own anger and acknowledge what we are feeling, it dissipates instantly – it's like taking the lid off a pressure cooker! The intensity of the emotion goes and we can process it with greater ease. This is far more effective and constructive than trying to keep a lid on it all!

Old anger which has not been expressed builds up within us. When something angers us in the present, we can feel powerless to express it, often letting resentment take its place. Or else we completely over-react to something in the present because of the underlying anger or rage that is under the surface. It is so important to heal ourselves by working through the backlog of anger and taking the necessary steps to let it go. There are many ways to communicate or express old anger, most of which are a part of the counselling process.

We can write about it, or write a letter to the person we are feeling anger towards. The letter can then be sent, burned, or ripped up, but not before you read it aloud. You can paint or draw it using colours. Anger can be expressed through movement, by walking, running or dancing, or even by punching pillows! Toddlers can teach us a thing or two about anger, as throwing a tantrum (preferably in your bathroom or bedroom and not in a supermarket aisle!) is a great way to express this emotion. With some of us, anger needs to be communicated in person, as was the case with me regarding both of my parents. I wouldn't recommend doing this without the support and advice of a counsellor as it can be difficult to revisit the past with someone who is in denial and may not be open to hearing what you have to say.

The most important thing to remember is this: anger that is unexpressed outside of ourselves expresses itself within us (as do all emotions). It doesn't vanish just because we don't express it. We hold it in our bodies and it finds expression inside us. We become victims of our own anger. I believe anger is one of many emotions that can cause us to become diseased when internalized. When we look at the word disease – dis-ease – that which is not at ease or not in harmony, it makes perfect sense. We must find positive ways to express our emotions outside of ourselves. Emotion is energy in motion (e-motion) and energy needs to flow. We must learn to express and communicate our feelings of anger (or shame, guilt, unforgiveness etc.), and then we must learn to let it go.

I had not just been angry with my father and my brothers. I was angry with my mother, for not protecting me, for burdening me with her problems from a young age, for not letting me express myself emotionally, for not listening to my needs and for wanting me to grow up before my time and rescue her from her life. I was angry with my sister for leaving me and for being irritable, moody and distant at times. I was angry with every member of my family and that is a lot of anger to have been bottling up internally. I was angry with life for being such a disappointment and with God for giving me such a bad deal and then abandoning me, as I thought. I'm very glad that I had the courage to let it go as I don't think I would be a very well person today if I hadn't! The counselling process helps us to uncover the emotions, layer by layer, until there are no more. Knowing this, I wasn't surprised that what lay underneath my anger was a lot of hurt and sadness. If I hadn't been hurt and sad, I wouldn't have been so angry.

I mentioned Kevin (my boyfriend of four years) earlier in my own life story. Kevin was both an alcoholic and a compulsive gambler from a very young age. I also mentioned that he had a difficult time growing up. His father used to go to the pub regularly, get drunk, come home and beat him, often using his belt buckle. I saw the scars Kevin had on his body, especially on his legs and knees. When he went for counselling some years later he shared these experiences, but was quick to defend his father, saying that he didn't know any better. Kevin was pulled up by the counsellor about this and was told that his father *did* know better. He was told that what his father did was wrong and knew it was wrong. Kevin was enraged at this realisation, and when he left the session he drove straight to his parent's house and proceeded to hit and kick his father to the ground. Thankfully, his father made a complete recovery.

Initially, and for quite some time after, Kevin was unrepentant about what he had done. He said he had taken his power back and let go of all his anger in the process. Later, he felt tremendous guilt and shame, and realised that what he had done was wrong too. Kevin's way of denying his anger was to not blame his father (it wasn't his fault). He probably blamed himself as children are so good at doing, so when he finally faced his anger, it was so overwhelming that it consumed him completely in that moment. He also didn't know how to express it any other way at the time. Thankfully, Kevin and his father made their peace with each other, but it took some time.

Kevin's story is not a typical one, but it does remind us that anger is a powerful force and needs to be released through positive expression. Anger that is denied will always find expression through negative channels. I believe that a lot of addictions, for example to food, drink, drugs, gambling, sex, pornography and prostitution, are expressions of anger. We cannot let go of the hurt and sadness and all of the other emotions that lie trapped within us until we unleash our anger.

For me, roaring into my pillow, writing, meditation, yoga, breathing, walking and painting are all ways that I am comfortable expressing anger. Sometimes I throw a tantrum too, which always makes me laugh!

Anger

Sick to my skin, it's this poison within;
It's filling me and killing me, wearing me down.
The colour is red, wild flashes in my head;
a deep burning rage, tight fisted and caged.

181

It catches in my throat; invisible hands grip and choke.
I am silenced once again, once again.
What can be done, what can be said?
When I am powerless,
confused and full of dread.
Punished for being angry,
Punished for being me; for rattling all the cages,
and for saying how I feel.
I am trapped – trapped instead of free,
as I rage inside, like the wild, stormy sea.

I so want to let it come,
But I'm afraid I'll come undone,
And so the loneliness goes on. . .
And on.

– Deirdre Brady

Chapter 9

Guilt and Shame

'Sugar and spice and all things nice – that's what little girls are made of...'

I mentioned this in my life story because I distinctly remember believing when I first heard this nursery rhyme that I wasn't made from anything nice at all. The 'slugs and snails and puppy dog tails' sounded more like my insides. From as young an age as I can remember, I felt different to other boys and girls my age and not in a good way. I thought that God must have made a mistake when he made me. There was no doubt in my mind that I was somehow bad, that I was inherently flawed; it was my secret and I couldn't tell anyone. I just knew it and lived in the fear that someone would find out. I didn't like making eye-contact with adults because I was sure that they would be able to see the badness – that I would be found out!

Why did I feel this way? Mary explained it to me one day in counselling. 'Children are like sponges,' she said. 'They soak up everything that is happening to them or around them.' She explained that children not only take responsibility for themselves, but take responsibility for everything that others say and do, because they do not have the discernment or the ability to separate their behaviour from others. They cannot differentiate between what is theirs and what isn't. If there is something happening that feels wrong, a child will automatically blame themselves and wonder what they have done to deserve their negative feelings. This is why, even when parents argue in front of a child, a child's self-worth and confidence is negatively affected.

In counselling, when I spoke about how I felt around my father from a very young age, I used the word 'sick' a lot. Bouncing on his knee made me feel sick and being in the car on my own with him made me feel sick. His voice, when it became low and husky, made me feel sick. I particularly remembered feeling sick when I saw my dad putting his hand up my friend's skirt in the front seat of his car. My counsellor Mary noticed that this incident in the car seemed to bother me particularly and asked me why. I had only remembered this incident after meeting with my cousins in Kildare. I recalled it with absolute clarity, which I couldn't say about most of my childhood. But even I wasn't sure why was it bothering me so much.

'Tell me all you can remember of that morning,' Mary said.

It was Saturday morning. It was the only thing that our dad ever did with us but he always acted differently, weirdly, when there were other children present. I always felt embarrassed and I didn't know why. I much preferred when we went with Sophie's Dad. Ann always sat in the front with Dad, I remembered that. On this particular day, I was sitting behind my father, by the window. When I looked through the gap in the seats I saw that my dad had his hand on Ann's bare leg and was rubbing it. I was shocked and horrified at the same time. Next, I saw him move his hand up her skirt and I felt my face get very hot and red. I felt a familiar sick feeling in my stomach and my head felt like it was going to explode. Then I looked out the window and I didn't remember any more.

I paused then, and my eyes were drawn down to the floor. 'What is it, Dee?' Mary said. 'What just happened there?' I was quiet for a moment, and then the tears started to fall.

'I looked away ... I looked out the window,' I said. 'I pretended that it wasn't happening, that I didn't see it. I could have done something ... I should have done something ... for Ann, but I did nothing. I should have helped her, but I just looked out the window.'

I was really sobbing now. I was feeling so much shame for what my father had done, but I was also feeling a huge amount of guilt for pretending that it wasn't happening. The sick feelings I had described were really feelings of shame and guilt. Through the counselling process, I came to understand and accept that I could have done nothing to help Ann, my cousin, or even myself. I was a child with no power. The person that was doing these things was not a stranger, but my father and he was the one with all the power. I was just a child who felt guilt and shame, sadness and confusion, every day. Now, as an adult, I could do something about these feelings. I could hand back the guilt and the shame. It wasn't my guilt or my shame. I began the slow process of learning to love and care about myself. As I let go of the self-loathing, I started to treat myself with kindness, patience, understanding and compassion. I began to heal. This guilt and shame around Ann came up a second time for me, some years later, and this is not uncommon either. The more we learn and grow, the more we can let go.

Guilt and shame can be so deeply embedded within us that we are not outwardly aware of their existence. Instead, we feel flawed with pervasive feelings of not being good enough and not being loveable. All of these feelings play out in the way that we behave in life. How we behave is an outward reflection of how we feel and think about ourselves. Creating guilt and shame in our lives is a consequence of growing up with these emotions and if I create shame and guilt in my life, it is because I have inner shame and guilt to acknowledge and work through The same way that if I create anger in my life, then I have inner anger to acknowledge and work through. If I have trust issues in my life, I have inner mistrust to acknowledge and work through. And so on ...

A good example of this from my own life would be the decision that I made not to tell the truth about who my son's father was. This lie, this deceit and this secret (all familiar feelings playing out in my life) created a huge amount of guilt and shame. It took me some time before I could face the consequences of this decision. I had to stop judging myself and find some good inside myself first, before I could look at my mistakes. Once I had stopped blaming myself for everything that had ever happened to me and see that I wasn't a bad person, I could open up to taking responsibility for my own choices and decisions. When we judge and blame and beat ourselves up, we can't even acknowledge or accept our actions or behaviour, never mind forgive ourselves. This keeps the real feelings of shame and guilt (the old feelings) locked away inside. Unfortunately, until a person is willing to look at themselves with love and self-acceptance and without judgment, they will stay in this circle of creation.

With shame and guilt being such a common consequence of child sexual abuse, there is often a strong association between these emotions and our sexuality, where the guilt and shame originated. Therefore, it is quite common that the guilt and shame that we have inside is played out in our sexual lives. I often cried after having casual sex, feeling overwhelmed with feelings of guilt and shame, never understanding why. And intimate sex, where love and sex both exist, can be so very confusing to a victim of sexual abuse, especially if their abuser was a loved one. This can manifest in our lives as promiscuity, inability to maintain an intimate relationship, infidelity, pornography and prostitution. When we let go of the feelings of guilt and shame that others were responsible for, it allows us then to stop recreating these feelings in our own lives.

Most of the guilt and shame that I had felt my whole life wasn't even mine, and when I finally realised this I could hear the words *I am good enough. I am loveable. I'm not bad.* The little girl inside me was finally able to begin to love herself.

I no longer try to change outer things.
They are simply a reflection.
I change my inner perception and
the outer reveals the beauty
so long obscured by my own attitude.
I concentrate on my inner vision and
find my outer view transformed.
I find myself attuned
to the grandeur of life and
in unison with the perfect order
of the Universe.

'Daily Word', From the *Book of Runes*, by Ralph Blum

Chapter 10

Letting the Tears Fall

I have cried so many tears in this lifetime – tears of relief, sadness, grief, anger, forgiveness, happiness and tears of achievement. The tears that came with self-acceptance and self-love and of realising that I was loved. Tears of letting go, of moving on and of freedom from pain; beautiful, healthy, healing tears.

For me, crying is about letting go. It is an ancient call of surrender. We are defenceless when we cry. We are vulnerable when we cry. We are soft when we cry. We can feel great love when we cry. We can feel very close to God when we cry. It's as if Heaven reaches out and embraces us when we cry. Most importantly, we heal when we cry.

The healing process is about revealing the layers of emotions as they come up, acknowledging and experiencing them, before moving on. Sadness and hurt came up for me time after time during my first two years of counselling and has come up many times since. There were times when I wondered if there would ever be an end to the hurt and the tears, but I kept going. After anger came sadness and hurt. After acceptance came sadness and hurt. When the shame and guilt were finally let go of, there was enormous sadness and hurt for all the years that I lived under a black cloud, never feeling good enough, and never feeling worthy of anything good.

There was more sadness for all the suffering that had come with believing that I was unlovable. This was even beyond anger – I felt absolute desolation and my bed became my retreat from life for a while. Where once I stretched out straight in bed, I curled up like a snail, back to the silence, the darkness and the security of the womb. Here I licked my wounds and cried deeply for the child within me. The child who had been so hurt, the child who had known such sadness. In this dark, quiet place of refuge, I found myself again. I felt an awareness of all the pain and suffering this wonderful planet endures. It was as if I had tapped into the consciousness of the world and through my pain, I found the love that lies at the heart of all suffering. I found God. I also found my spiritual self, the part of me that IS God. I found my light in the darkness and knew then that I need never suffer again. I may know sadness, hurt, grief or anger, but I became aware that I was not just the experiences of my life: I was so much more than that. My life had been my choosing and increased compassion, understanding and forgiveness had been my lesson and my privilege to learn. Love could be my motivation, not suffering.

Now I had an inner strength that would never leave me. My tears were tears of joy, freedom, understanding and love. I found forgiveness with all of my being. What I had learned was so much more important than what I had experienced. The greatest lesson I have learned so far is that love is all that really matters and love is a choice. I still feel sadness and hurt sometimes. I still feel anger and resentment too. There are times when I feel awkward, different and that I don't belong. The difference now is that I know I am not alone.

There is great freedom in being able to express whatever you are feeling, let it go and move on, to be able to be still and quiet within yourself. I have seen many people who have tried to run away from their pain, and spend their lives running around in circles, unaware that they are carrying their hurt with them all the time. Revisiting sadness and hurt does not mean experiencing it all over again, like opening up a wound, but rather we experience it as we let it go. Imagine that sadness and hurt were locked up in a cage inside you, only now you had a key and could unlock the cage, release the feelings and let them go. When our childhood feelings are locked up inside, so too is the child who felt those feelings. This is where the term 'inner child' comes from. We all want to experience this emotional freedom and we can, with a little courage, determination and love.

I have one word of caution with regards to emotional pain (or indeed any pain): do not become over-identified with it. The popular saying, 'pain is inevitable, suffering is optional,' is important to remember. Pain knocks on all of our doors at some point in our lives, and if we can accept it, without wallowing in it endlessly, we do not need to suffer. Suffering comes when we fight, ignore or try to anaesthetise pain. Suffering also happens when we see ourselves as victims or martyrs in our lives. I made that mistake for a time in my own life. I had become so used to being sad, always becoming emotional in counselling or at workshops that I began to see myself as 'Deirdre of the Sorrows.' I had plenty of justification but it wasn't helpful! When I read *Chakras and Their Archetypes* by Ambika Wauters, I began to see my victim mentality at work. Eckhart Tolle's book *A New Earth: Create a Better Life* also resonated with me. Eckhart talks about the pain body and how it can be a negative force in one's life. He describes the pain body as 'the remnants of pain left behind by every strong negative emotion that is not fully faced, accepted, and then let go of ... consisting of not just childhood pain, but also painful emotions that were added to it later in adolescence and during adult life.' Eckhart explains how the pain body is addicted to unhappiness. I understood this completely, even if I didn't like it: unhappiness was for me a familiar way of life for so long and it was an easy coat to wear. I became aware of the need to consciously choose love and happiness every day in my life.

> *Love, to be real,*
> *It must cost,*
> *It must hurt,*
> *It must empty us of self.*
> – Mother Teresa.

> *He who loves*
> *Has conquered the world*
> *And has no fear of losing anything.*
> *True love is an act of total surrender.*
> – Paolo Coelho

Chapter 11

The Grief of a Lost Childhood

Two weeks after my mother died in 2004, I met Terry, a family acquaintance who had lost her husband Pat a few years previously. It was Christmas week and I was really feeling the loss of my mom. Terry consoled with me over my loss and then she said to me:

'I'm going to give you some advice, which I hope will serve you well. Don't try to get over the loss of someone you love. You never will.' Great, I thought, that's just what I needed to hear. But she went on to say, 'You're not meant to get over anyone and you'll fail miserably if you try. No, instead, ask God to help you to accept your loss and come to terms with your grief, so that you can learn to live with it. That is the only way forward.'

Of course she was right and I was glad of her wise words. Obviously, we don't need to believe in God to find acceptance, but Terry knew that I did believe in God (even if I didn't have her religious faith).

The advice came to mind when I was thinking about writing this chapter. How did I get over my lost childhood? I haven't really. I have learned acceptance on many levels. I have learned to accept that I do not have a single happy memory from my childhood that involves my family; not yet anyway. I have learned to accept and love each family member for who they are, even if I don't always like them! I have learned to accept that my family have been torn apart and that my only sister lives five thousand miles away. I have learned to accept the difficult relationship I had with my mother growing up, her neglect of my emotional needs and her conditional love. Accepting my father was a long and difficult process. In accepting him, I had to let go of the father of my dreams and that proved very difficult indeed. I must have fantasized many times about my dream father: he was strong and larger than life, and when he held my hand, or held me in his arms, I felt so safe and so loved. He was kind and gentle and loved to hear about my day and my adventures. He adored me and made me feel special. I loved spending time with him and being the apple of his eye. I had to let go of the father of my dreams and the loss was devastating, as was the loss of my innocence. But I got back up again; I survived and became stronger for it.

There was a time in my life when I was lost. I believed that I had no value, was unlovable and I stopped caring for myself. I can't say I stopped loving myself, because I had never loved myself, only my own choices in life began to reflect this reality. I felt as though I had already died in some way, that I had let go of the will to live. When I look back, I can understand why: my world was full of misery and hardship, other people kept hurting me and I kept hurting myself. There was never any good news, only bad. I didn't trust anyone, including myself. This left me nowhere to turn (or so I thought), and my life became more bleak and hopeless every day.

A few months after I came down to Tipperary, I found myself in a quaint little church with beautiful stained glass windows. Feeling like a shadow of who I once was, I got down on my knees and prayed for help. Almost instantly the church filled with the most beautiful golden light I had ever seen. I looked up and saw that the sun was shining through the stained glass windows, pouring light down on me and I felt its embrace. My whole body filled up with this light and I felt my heart being embraced. In that moment, I knew that I wasn't alone. I felt the presence of Christ and knew he could feel all the pain and sadness within me. I knew he had been with me through everything and had been waiting patiently for me to call on him. He showed me the way back to God and to my self. When I became aware of God's presence in my heart, I felt the fatherly love that I had so longed for and it was very healing.

I could never replace what I had lost in my life. I could, however, be thankful for all that I did have growing up. I could acknowledge all that I had learned. I have a love of animals, of nature and of the sea, that stem from my childhood. I found peace during my life in the whispering wind, the crashing waves, the sheltered rock pools that fascinated me (and still do). God may have been the giant horse chestnut tree that I climbed regularly and sat in for hours as a child, feeling safe and hidden. I have a love of travelling, of music and of reading that also come from my youth. I have learned to be grateful every day for everything in my life. I am grateful for the love and connection I now have with my sister. I am grateful for the love that my brothers and I share. I am grateful for the love that my mother and I will always share, a love that goes beyond any lifetime and I am grateful for the closeness that we shared in the last years of her life. I am grateful for the friends that I had growing up and the friends that I have today. I am grateful to everyone who has helped me on my journey through life. I am most grateful for my own wonderful family: my husband Jimmy, my three amazing children and our happy, harmonious home. My life experiences have made me stronger, wiser and more courageous. I have become more compassionate and more understanding. I have learned patience, perseverance, tolerance, kindness and discernment (all still very much a work in progress!). The greatest gifts I have are the relationships I have with myself and the relationship I have with God. Once I take responsibility for my life, my needs and my happiness, then I have balance in my life and all my other relationships are more enriched and more positive. I have learned the importance of surrendering everything and not to let myself get bogged down by life's circumstances. I ask God and the Universe to help when I feel under pressure or disheartened in any way.

What about grief? I believe that grief is a natural emotion and when we lose someone or something precious from our physical world we need to process our grief. When I had my astrology reading done, I was told that I had 'deep, personal grief' that I had not finished working through but would continue to heal through my life's work. I wasn't sure what this meant and it took me some time to figure it out. When we have years of unprocessed grief, it can take years to heal. It can also shape our lives and our destiny. I believe that grief inspires and motivates us. Accepting grief as part of our life's journey deepens us and connects us to what is real. It strengthens us and helps us to know ourselves and understand each other better. We cannot force grief, just as we cannot force the rain to fall. Yet, like the rain, we can wake up in the morning and it is there, waiting to be relinquished. It is important to accept it when it does come. We also have a need to teach what we have learned so that we can continue to heal that part of us. Grief reminds us of what it is we need to do and allows us to do it with compassion and humility.

Grief

Sometimes it comes so gently, quietly,
like the rain falling softly.
Stepping out into it is easy,
surrendering to the gentle quenching.
Other times it lashes hard on the window,
demanding attention: colder and less welcome,
yet exhilarating, cleansing to feel.
Sometimes darkness for days – weeks –
no sign of light: only the knowing
that day follows night, and darkness
is always followed by the light.
Look for the gift, for it will come,
Like the dancing rainbow and the morning sun.

– Deirdre Brady

Chapter 12

Being Empty and Still Again

Once upon a time, I didn't like my own company very much. I was lonely and felt very alone when I was by myself. Now I can be with myself, which is a very different place to be. My trip to Kilkee in County Clare in 2008, on the advice of my counsellor Mary, was the first time in my life that I had chosen to go somewhere on my own. I was a little bit afraid but also excited. I was venturing into unknown territory in every way. I felt so free and my journey ahead was full of possibility. The evening that I arrived in Kilkee, the sun was setting over the Atlantic Ocean and I saw a kaleidoscope of colours filling the sky. I couldn't wait to walk the cliffs and explore this beautiful place that seemed to welcome me. My weekend was magical: the sun shone for me, the breeze whispered to me, even the dolphins came to see me. I sat for hours on the cliffs each day, in no hurry to be anywhere else. There was nowhere else I wanted to be; I was still, I was peaceful and I was so very happy to be in my own company. Someone said to me once, *you have to find the soul mate in yourself before you can find it in another.* I found my inner soul mate that weekend, and will always remember it as a very special moment in my life. Getting there had been hard work, but it had been so worth it.

For those of us who have known a lot of loss and sadness growing up, it feels almost as if there is a hole inside us. In my experience, this hole was about what was missing, about what I didn't have. If I were to call that hole something, it would be 'lack'. There was a lack of love and of nurturance. There was a lack of safety and stability. There was a lack of values, a lack of emotional support and a lack of guidance. That's a frightening hole to look into. As adults, a lot of us try to fill it up with other stuff. Nothing works for long and the hole begins to feel like a bottomless pit that can never be filled. It seems to get bigger and darker as time goes on. There is only one solution, and that is to jump right in.

There is always a leap of faith involved in the process of counselling, healing or self-change, but it is always a rewarding one. Faith can really help us to take this leap, whether it's faith in ourselves, faith in a higher power, faith in humanity or faith in God. Otherwise our minds persuade us not to go there, not to take a chance when we don't know the outcome. We need to believe that we can overcome our fears. We need to get out of our minds when it comes to the big things in our lives and make decisions with our hearts – the mind will always find an excuse or a question. Some of us need to explore our beliefs a little further before moving forward into the unknown. Others walk away from the edge and back to their familiar and painful lives. Remember that if we're never out of our comfort zone, we're never growing. We have to push ourselves sometimes, stretch and expand into new territory. If we don't, our world will remain a small and limited place.

The first thing I realised, when I took my leap of faith, was that the walls were not as high and the hole was not as deep as I had imagined. Fear had caused an illusion of some magnitude! There was no bottomless pit that I would never be able to climb out of. It is true what is said about fear, that 'there is nothing to fear but fear itself.' Another fear I had was that I would be overwhelmed by my feelings. The truth was that I could actually set them free. There was a paradox here, in that where I thought there would be darkness, there was light. So often in the past I had searched for light and found darkness. Where I thought there would be loneliness, I found solitude.

Now I could experience being empty and feel a stillness within me that I had not experienced before. I did not need to run away from myself anymore. Fear, which had been such a force in my life, was now replaced by freedom. Relief quickly turned to gratitude. Peace and serenity came with acceptance. My faith and belief in myself and in God deepened. Where I had felt out of balance, I now felt very centred and grounded. I still grieve – there will always be something to let go of. Every time I learn something new and grow stronger and wiser, something old surfaces, like an old weed, to be let go of. It is a beautiful process and it's all about letting it flow and trusting in the process of life. Mindfulness is a wonderful way of living and helps me to be really present in my life. When we connect to our breath, to nature (the cycles and seasons), we realise that life is all about cycles and about letting go. We don't see trees trying to hold on to their leaves: they let go, in the knowledge that there is nothing to do in each moment but to surrender and the cycle of life will continue. There is an intelligence at work that is far greater than our individual selves.

Every day now, I take time to be still. I empty my mind and I listen. I listen to my heart, to my inner knowing: to God. In the silence, I can ask a question and receive an answer. Sometimes, I have to wait a while, but I always get one. I can better understand why it is that I may be struggling with something or someone in my life. Sometimes, in the stillness, I feel elevated, as if I am standing on the cliffs in Kilkee, with the ocean spread out under me and a blue sky overhead. The clarity I find is a real gift. Other times I struggle to empty my mind and feel distracted by every sound, but that's part of life too, and that's where perseverance comes in.

Speaking of God, I'd like to take a moment to share my personal beliefs about what God means to me, as this has changed and evolved over the years. I don't believe that God is a person or a single being; I believe that God is love and light (light being wisdom or consciousness). The Universe, I believe, is a living creation, made with the energy of love. Maybe the Universe is God and maybe there are other Universes. I don't know and I don't have all the answers, but I do know that everything is connected and as we are evolving, we are becoming more aware of the interconnectedness of all of life. I don't believe in religions as they only cause division (some more so than others). Some religions also seem to create discrimination and inequality between the sexes. I believe that there have been many enlightened beings who have lived on this planet: Jesus, Moses, Mohammad and Buddha who inspired religions and many others like Nelson Mandela, Albert Einstein, Marie Curie, Martin Luther King, William Shakespeare, Leonardo da Vinci, Rosa Parks, Mother Theresa, Anne Frank, Florence Nightingale, Mahatma Gandhi and many, many more. Religious teachings are very similar, with values of love, forgiveness, humility, generosity and compassion at their core, so why can't we all get along?

I don't claim to understand God, but I can liken it to a drop of water and the ocean. I am both the drop of water and the ocean (because I am part of the whole and yet individual). I am a part of God and God is a part of me. So are you, and therefore we are all connected and all part of the whole. I do have a personal connection with Jesus because he came to me and showed me the way when I was suffering. I have had experiences with many ascended masters, angels and guides from other cultures and religions as well. If I were to choose a religion that comes closest to my beliefs it would be Hinduism, in that I believe in reincarnation and Karma. I have also noticed that 'New Age' is a term used to describe a more common view of spirituality today, which is holistic, inclusive and more representative of people's beliefs in the modern world. I love the Buddhist traditions of meditation and simplicity, appreciating the transience of life and the value of humility. What's important about any religion or ideology is that its foundation be based on love and not fear, as well as compassion, tolerance, acceptance, forgiveness and non-judgement. I certainly don't have all the answers, but though I might not understand what God is in my head, I know who God is in my heart.

Silence is the language of God.
All else is a poor translation.

– Rumi

Chapter 13

Self-love and Acceptance

Loving and accepting myself has been the hardest and most challenging part of the healing process for me. The saddest and most damaging legacy of my unhappy childhood is the struggle I have had to love and accept myself completely and unconditionally.

By the time I had completed psychotherapy (for the first time), I had a lot of work done. I had learned self-forgiveness, self-respect, self-esteem and maybe even self-like. I also had a much greater understanding of my life. But I hadn't learned how to love and accept myself unconditionally. I could see very clearly how my lack of self-love had shaped my life and the decisions and choices I had made in the past. I could see very clearly how my lack of self-love directly influenced my relationships in the past and my choice of partners. The beginning of loving myself came to me in a spiritual way. The first time in my adult life that I felt the presence of Jesus was, as I mentioned earlier, in the lovely church in Tipperary. Later, I also experienced God's healing love through the power of Reiki. Without God in my life, I don't think I would fully understand what unconditional love is. When I first experienced Reiki, I felt closeness with God, an intimacy that has allowed me to feel this immense love for me and for everyone. If I could be so loved by an outside force – that knew me and understood me intimately – then I could love myself too. This was the beginning of self-love and self-acceptance and I am still on my journey. That connection and closeness is there for me and is with me every day that I remember to engage with it. The days that I am struggling are the days when I think I am all alone, when I forget that I belong and am a part of life.

It has always been so easy to blame myself, to feel not good enough or not worthy. It's what I knew for so long, so I have to remember to consciously work at negating my old ways of thinking. I always had impossible expectations of myself, which made accepting myself difficult as I could never lived up to my expectations. In my youth I had an attractive body, reasonable good looks and I loved getting reactions from others, particularly men. It affirmed me in some way; I was acceptable, even if it was just in a physical way. I didn't feel beautiful inside and was therefore giving my power away, looking for assurances from others.

Now I am older and have three children and my physical body is not what it used to be. At first I found this difficult and became very critical of my physical self focusing on the negatives: my sagging breasts, my scars and my stretch marks. These negative thoughts were exacerbated by feelings of guilt. How could I be so vain when I had three beautiful, perfectly healthy children that I was so grateful for? The guilt led to feelings of self-loathing and not self-loving. I was also afraid that my husband would no longer find me attractive and therefore no longer love me. I had to dig deeper within myself and start acknowledging my wonderful body and the miracle that I am. It helped me to value my inner beauty and the qualities and virtues that make me special and unique. I began to give thanks every day for every part of me, inside and out. I now accept the effect that children, age and gravity are having on my body and I consciously choose to love myself every day, stretch marks and all! I remind myself to let go of the negative thinking and focus on loving myself. I do not have to be perfect to be lovable. It's all about feeling and knowing I am worthy of love, as are we all.

Society puts a lot of pressure on women to have perfect bodies and women are sexualised through television, the film industry, advertising, magazines and in newspapers. Average women's figures and sizes are rarely seen and this gives many the belief that they are not attractive. The biggest burden is often felt by teenagers and young women who are so vulnerable and impressionable to the world around them. Society is teaching them to have a sexual identity at a young age when many have not even learned self-respect and self-esteem. We need to get back to real values again and help our young people to find and express their talents, their creativity and their value.

The commitment to loving and accepting ourselves unconditionally is the single most important decision we can make as human beings, bringing healing, peace and joy into our lives. When I had my astrology reading done, I was told that I need to consciously love myself every day. This took a while to put into practice, but now I tell myself daily that I deserve love, health, joy, abundance, success, friendship and peace of mind. Loving myself has brought me so much peace and happiness and it is really worth the commitment that it takes to consciously practice it every day.

When I first started using affirmations many years ago, I thought my whole life would change in a few weeks and I would never need to use them again – how naive of me! Self-love is a lifelong commitment to support, nurture and nourish myself as I continue to grow and learn. Using positive loving affirmations every day really help in the process of self-love and acceptance The following affirmations are general and very effective in helping to negate old thinking patterns:

I love and approve of myself.
I love and accept myself.
I am willing to change and grow.
Life is a joy and filled with love.
I am always safe.
I love and appreciate myself and others.
I give myself permission to be all that I can be.
I deserve the very best in life.
I prosper wherever I turn.
I am safe and I am love.
All is well in my world.
Everything I need comes to me in the perfect time,
space and sequence.

Affirmations need to be said aloud, repeated three times each and said at least twice a day. They are very effective and greatly aid the process of self-love, change and ultimately healing. Louise Hay has written many beautiful books and her bestselling book, *You Can Heal Your Life,* is full of wonderful affirmations.

What is unconditional love? Well, let me first tell you what I believe *con*ditional love is: *con*ditional love is being loved *if* – *if* you do things my way, *if* you behave, *if* you don't make demands on me, *if* you let me control you, *if* you don't leave me. Conditional love is love that is often withdrawn and is used to control and manipulate. It is a fear-based love. When a child grows up with conditional love, they grow up believing that they are only lovable sometimes, at best. The rest of the time they feel that they are not good enough, or not worthy of love. To undo these deep-rooted beliefs takes time, patience and a real desire to change old patterns and move forward.

Imagine if you had been told, or were made feel as a child, that you didn't deserve to be loved. What if you were made to feel this every day for fifteen or twenty years. Of course, you would believe it to be true, and would tell yourself so – every day – in many ways. Imagine then, if one day you realised that you *did* deserve to be loved, that you were always deserving of love and deserved to be shown love every day. Would it not take some time, or even a lifetime, to negate the old pattern of thinking about what you believed to be the truth? It does take time and it is so important to take time every day to remind ourselves that we are lovable, loving and loved. It is important for anyone who has grown up with conditional love, or lack of love, to do this.

So what does unconditional love mean? I have heard the term used so many times but rarely defined. To me, it is the ability to give love freely without reservations or conditions: it is loving with total acceptance. Unconditional love is practiced by those who believe in the infinite supply and abundance of love – and not the notion that we have a small amount of love inside us and we have to be careful who we give it to. Love is a very powerful energy, all by itself. Love flows and when we allow it in, it heals us. We can be open and receptive to love and draw it in to ourselves, or we can fear love or continue believing that we do not deserve love in our lives. This blocks love from coming to us. When we become aware of how infinite and endless love is, it allows us to really embrace ourselves and our spirituality.

The most important thing I have learned about unconditional love is that we must be willing to love *ourselves* unconditionally, before we can love others unconditionally. In other words, we cannot give to others what we do not have for ourselves. Therefore, if we love some things about ourselves and don't love our flaws or weaknesses, we are loving ourselves *conditionally*. We are also pushing away parts of us that we do not like or accept, and this creates division within us. How can we be whole, or complete, if we are pushing parts of ourselves away? Being whole is not about being perfect, but is about loving every part of ourselves – embracing everything – flaws and all!

When we are willing to love and accept ourselves completely, we can let go of fear and can forgive ourselves our faults and failings. What we deny about ourselves – what we choose not to love – we cannot change. We don't have to be perfect and we don't have to like everything about ourselves, but we do have to love ourselves, flaws and all. Loving ourselves completely gives us the ability and the freedom to look at every part of ourselves and accept our emotions without judgement. Most of our flaws and shortcomings are fear-based and require a compassionate, understanding and loving approach.

Are you patient and kind with yourself, or do you blame, judge or put yourself down? Do you support and give encouragement, or do you judge or criticize yourself and others harshly? What is your 'self-talk' like? Would you speak to a child this way? When you look in the mirror, do you find something to criticise, or do you smile and give thanks for the miracle that is you! If you find that this is too much of a stretch, imagine that every time you looked in the mirror, you were looking at a child (a real one). Imagine that child having to endure your endless criticism and chastisement – would that child be happy? Would that child flourish and feel confident and loved? Remember, we all have a child inside that just wants to be loved and accepted, so smile – give yourself a complement – it's feels good to love yourself!

If there is something that you don't like, you can choose to change it. You can decide to practice non-judgement, acceptance, kindness and compassion and when you slip back into old patterns, you can notice it, forgive yourself and move on. If there are patterns in our thinking or behaviour which we don't understand or don't know how to change, it is important to look for help. Once we are willing to make a commitment to helping and healing ourselves, all things become possible.

Self-love and acceptance do not always come easy and we all struggle with different aspects of ourselves. The people that we share our lives with also help to mirror our inner struggles and conflicts so that we can see them more clearly. When we have conflict or disharmony in any of our relationships, we are being shown something of ourselves which we have not healed. It is always important to look for the lesson in any situation or relationship. The more willing we are to learn and heal, the quicker we can move through the disharmony and find peace again.

For example, about a year ago, I found the company of two people in my extended family difficult at times. They irritated me. I struggled with this for a while as I didn't understand why I felt so irritated. Then I found an affirmation that helped me: 'I am willing to release that part of me which is irritated, when I think of you.' It worked beautifully because it made me take responsibility for my feelings, instead of blaming the individuals who I thought had *made* me feel irritated. Once I had taken responsibility for feeling angry, I began to understand why. It was completely about me and about something I had not forgiven in myself. It was a wonderful lesson to learn.

Finally, we cannot love and accept ourselves completely without getting to know and understand ourselves better. It's a great idea to get away by yourself every now and then: a day trip to the sea, a yoga or meditation retreat, or a quiet weekend of reflection, meditation, walking and writing are just a few suggestions. The better we get to know ourselves, the more we learn trust and discernment and we cultivate a better relationship with the most important person in our lives – ourselves!

For me, I have a morning routine which gets my day off to a really positive start. Most mornings, I start with my yoga (or some gentle stretching) and my morning prayers. I ground myself, centre myself in my heart and take time to be still, to breathe and to listen. I ask myself how I am feeling. I can then allow expression to whatever feelings that are there, and I begin by acknowledging them. I notice what I have been thinking about and I surrender my thoughts. It is my favourite time of the day and it sets me up for the rest of the day. Being heart-centred is vital for my well-being. When I keep my awareness in my heart, I am most balanced. If I am out of balance, it is always because I haven't taken time, or because I am not listening to God or to my higher self.

Any time I have struggled in my life, it was because I wasn't listening to my spiritual nature. It wasn't intentional: it was a by-product of my need to control whatever crisis was happening in my life, instead of asking for help and guidance when I needed it most. I have learned to surrender (most of the time) whatever is going on in my life and now I ask for guidance along the way. What I have found wonderful is that I am much calmer and family life is much more harmonious when I surrender something instead of trying to control it. When I try to control outcomes, worry and fear constantly get in the way.

I spoke of fear in Chapter 6 and our need to overcome it, but what is fear? I have heard it said that there is only love and fear and that every other emotion is just an offshoot. It is also widely believed that fear is the opposite of love, the flip-side, if you like. Yet, fear is also an illusion, as it exists only if we believe in it. The more we choose love, the less we believe in fear. I was a great believer in fear growing up and the more I believed in fear, the more it played out in my life. Now I focus on love all the time, which means I cannot focus on fear. The following two diagrams express it most clearly:

FEAR

↓

Denial	Anger	Guilt/Shame	Loss
↓	↓	↓	↓
Judgmental	Unforgiving	Self-hatred	Despair
Disharmony	Loathing	Victimhood	Loneliness
↓	↓	↓	↓
Suppress Emotions	Resentment	Blame	Feeling Worthless
Bitterness	Illness	Dishonesty	Unhappiness
↓	↓	↓	↓
Negative Relationship with Self/Others		Mistrust of Self/Others	
Addictive/Compulsive Behaviour		Controlling/Manipulative Behaviour	

LOVE

↓

Acceptance	Gratitude	Surrender	Trust
↓	↓	↓	↓
Compassion	Joy	Personal Power	Freedom
Forgiveness	Vision	Wisdom	Purity
Mercy	Abundance	Grace	Adoration
↓	↓	↓	↓
Harmony	Happiness	Peace	Protection
Unity	Creativity	Prosperity	Understanding
↓	↓	↓	↓
Good Relationship with Self/Others		Success	Intimacy
Integrity	Honesty	Trust	Peace

It has taken quite some time to be able to say that I love and accept myself unconditionally, and to really believe it. Now I am building on that love and acceptance every day and so can you. Be in your heart – listen to the wisdom that resides there and get to know your real self, not the incessant voice of your mind. And when you have a decision or a choice to make in life, ask of yourself: is this choice based on love or fear? Always choose love.

In the solitude of the heart
eternal silence sings:
and the song he sings
is a song of joy
that tells of the love of the singer.

Longing for you, dear God,
I find you
and, finding
long for you all the more.

Two voices are heard
in the stillness of the heart:
one, noisy and insistent, is mine:
The other whispers:
Be still and know that I am God.

Extract from 'Listening to Silence'
– Canice Egan, S.J.

Chapter 14

Forgiveness and the Cycle of Healing

'*Unforgiveness* is like drinking *poison* yourself and waiting for the other person to die.' – Marianne Williamson.

When I was outlining the chapters of this book, I wondered why I left forgiveness towards the end. Forgiveness was very important to me and was an integral part of my healing – I thought I would want to shout about it from the start! But it was only when I finished the chapter on self-love and acceptance that I realised why. I had been willing to forgive everyone else in my life, but it was only when I began to love and accept myself that I could finally forgive *myself.*

It felt great forgiving everyone and letting go of all of the hurt, sadness and anger created by those who had hurt me. It didn't dawn on me that I needed to forgive myself, even though I had blamed myself for everything all my life, as so many of us do. I believe that most of the pain I felt as a result of having been abused as a child was because I blamed myself. I believe that most children do the same. That is what keeps us silent about it. At some level of my being, I was still angry with myself. It was only my willingness to love and accept myself every day that allowed me to let go of the self-blame and forgive myself complete. One thing I have learned recently is this: self-love is a choice, self-acceptance is a choice and forgiveness is a choice, based on our willingness to love and accept ourselves.

I looked up the Oxford Dictionary for the word 'forgive' and the meaning given is to 'cease to feel angry or resentful towards'. This brings me back to what I have always believed about forgiveness. We heal ourselves when we forgive and we hurt ourselves when we don't. Forgiveness is an act of self-love and really has very little to do with the person who has caused the hurt. We must be willing to forgive others for our own sake, because we don't want to remain angry and resentful. I read recently from a book called *Courage to Change* (an excellent Al-Anon book) about a person's views on forgiveness. I thought it was wonderfully put: 'I think of forgiveness as a scissors. I use it to cut the strings of resentment that bind me to a problem or past hurt. By releasing resentment, I set myself free.'

Forgiveness is a process like any other. When we become willing to forgive, we begin the process. One day, often sometime later, we wake up and realise that we have found that state of forgiveness. I remember saying for a long time that I was willing to forgive my father and thought that I had forgiven him. Yet I knew the very moment when I had completely forgiven him – I felt it – and it was so much more than just saying words; it was a state of being. It felt like I had been gifted freedom, love, grace, gratitude and understanding. I felt it again more recently when I realised that I had forgiven myself completely too.

Another valuable lesson I have learned is not to take other people's behaviour or their decisions personally.

Children take everything personally because they do not have the discernment to do otherwise, especially when a child's boundaries and sense of self have been damaged. If a parent is angry, distant or distracted, moody or unhappy, it becomes the child's fault. Every emotion and every argument is felt and owned by that child. This is how a child learns to focus on fear. If they are surrounded by negative emotions and negative behaviour, this is what they feel and what they learn as normal. Alternatively, when a child is brought up in a loving family with positive behaviour all around them, love is what they focus on because love is what they feel. So you could say that children are natural victims of love or fear.

When children grow up and do not learn to detach from the behaviour and fear-based emotions of others, they remain victims of that behaviour throughout their lives. As they have learned to focus on fear instead of love, they form belief systems based on fear and negativity, instead of love. Their thinking becomes contaminated by fear, which traps them in a cycle of negativity. It's painful enough to let go of a relationship without blaming ourselves entirely for its downfall. When we blame ourselves for everything that is 'wrong' in our lives, we cause so much unnecessary pain. Until we learn to separate ourselves from others' behaviour and beliefs, we will continue to hurt.

What has this got to do with forgiveness? Everything really, because when we remain victims of other people's behaviour or decisions, we continue to blame ourselves. We take it personally, which reaffirms what we learned growing up: 'It's my fault, I'm not good enough, why can't I make him/her/things better? I'm a failure, I knew I would be let down again, I don't deserve love/happiness/success' and so on. When we learn detachment and we stop taking everything personally, we stop blaming ourselves. We learn not to judge and we do not feel the same level of anger, resentment or pain. We can observe others' behaviour without the need to own it or fix it or change it. I know that the choices and decisions of the people closest to us can have a huge impact on our lives. This is where trust comes in; trust that there is something we need to learn through adversity or change. If someone makes a poor decision or choice, based on a lack of self-love, and that decision impacts on others, it's important not to take their decisions or choices personally. *How could he/she do this to me*, is a typical response, which just puts us in victim mode. It's not about us, it's primarily about them – they have done this to themselves first and foremost.

When my first serious relationship with my boyfriend Peter ended, the pain and the total devastation I felt was almost unbearable. I will never forget it and nobody else understood, particularly my friends. Why couldn't I just put it behind me? Why couldn't I get on with my life? Why did my life become so meaningless, so empty and miserable? Simply because I blamed myself and this opened up older and much more painful wounds. I wasn't good enough and that was why he left me. I wasn't good enough and that was why he came back and used me for sex. I had tried to prove them all wrong, but it turned out that they (my fears and beliefs about myself) had to be right after all. It *was* my fault: *Everything* had been my fault, I wasn't lovable and I obviously didn't deserve to be loved. No wonder I felt so devastated. No wonder I could hardly bear the pain I felt. No wonder

I stopped caring about myself. Of course my friends could not understand – I didn't understand at the time. They had all known rejection of some sort or another – jobs, college, boyfriends, but they got back up again. Their worlds didn't stop turning because they had self-esteem and self-respect and because they grew up feeling and knowing they were loved and valued – I didn't.

Detaching from others with love, looking at my own thinking and beliefs, letting go of the past (bit by bit), taking responsibility for myself (my choices and decisions) and allowing others to take responsibility for their choices and decisions, has given me great healing and has changed my life immeasurably. Focusing on love instead of fear and finding forgiveness for everyone (especially myself) has elevated me and my life to a new level. I know that no matter what happens in my life now, I will not stop loving myself. I know that if I make a mistake, I will forgive myself and be patient, understanding and compassionate with myself. I know that making mistakes is a part of life and I trust that I will learn something new every time. I have learned so much and I am grateful to all my teachers, good and bad. Life gives us the opportunities to learn and to grow and I am so grateful that I have come through some very difficult times in my life, that I have not only survived, but have become strengthened by it. My life's experiences have enriched my life, helping me to become more positive, more loving, more giving, more understanding, more patient, more compassionate, more generous, more trusting and more forgiving and tolerant. I have transformed my life, but still have a long way to go – at least I've learned to enjoy the ride!

I am writing this book in the hope that my life experiences can help others to overcome their past, rather than be defined by it. I hope that my story can help others to find love within themselves and others. I work with groups regularly and often come across people in pain – some in extraordinary pain. I can relate to their pain, I understand it and I'm not afraid of it. This in itself can bring healing, but my most important message, and the one that transforms lives, is the simple willingness to love, accept and forgive oneself. Through my workshops, courses and healing sessions (and hopefully, now, my writing), I feel so honoured and privileged to be able to help others – it makes it all worthwhile. Who would have thought that my worst nightmares, could have become my greatest gifts?

The Message

I climbed through the dark night,
I stumbled and I fell;
caught up in brambles,
nettles and thorns as well.
I cried and I bled,
while despair filled my head:
would my heart not let go,
of the light that it sought;
my life would not come to naught.
So I followed my heart – all else had failed,
through anger and sadness; wind and rain.

Yes I found my light,
and that wasn't the end:
in showing the world,
my sense of deserving came.
Yes, I found my light,
and the first lesson learned,
was to share it with others –
my sisters and brothers,
and heal all over again.

– Deirdre Brady

Chapter 15

Practicing Mindfulness and Positivity

Part of my healing journey involved reading spiritual and self-help books by writers such as Louise Hay, Doreen Virtue, M. Scott Peck, Neale Donald Walsch, Deepak Chopra, Inna Segal, Eckhart Tolle, Caroline Myss, Marianne Williamson and many more. I learned a lot about the importance of positive thinking, meditation, examining my belief systems and patterns of thinking. I began to explore what God meant to me and I developed a more personal relationship with God and with nature. Time spent alone in nature was where I felt most connected to life, when I felt most spiritual, when I felt myself expand and become part of all of life – this is where the magic happens for me. When I realised that the air around me was not just empty space, but that the gentle breeze could whisper to me, or the wild wind roar, always with something to say, I began to listen. While reading Carl Jung's *Memories, Dreams, Reflections*, I found someone who was expressing the same sentiments in a way that I could really understand and with more eloquence than I had ever been able to. Jung wrote:

In fact it seemed to me that the high mountains, the
rivers, lakes, trees, flowers and animals, far better
exemplified the essence of God than men...
Here nothing separated man from God; indeed, it
was as though the human mind looked down upon
Creation simultaneously with God.

Finally, someone else was putting into words what I had always felt.

I also began to pay attention to my thinking and noticed the negative patterns that were there. I could be inflexible and found it easy to blame others. I lacked discernment at times and I was judgemental too – always quick to find the faults and failings in others. It made me feel better about myself to find that everyone else was flawed too, but this only made me feel worse about myself – how could I bring out the best in others, and in myself, when I was looking for the negative and not the positive. Once I understood that I had picked up this habit because of my own lack of self-worth – finding fault with others was a way that I could feel more 'normal' – I realised that I could focus on the positive qualities in myself and others instead and create a new positive habit instead. When I look for the good in people, I generally find it and this is a far more positive way of living my life. Loving myself meant that I don't have to be perfect and neither does anyone else.

When we are making progress and moving forward in our lives, it becomes easier to accept what we cannot change (namely the past and other people) and focus instead on what we can change instead – ourselves. By looking at our beliefs, our thinking patterns and any negative patterns of behaviour, we can begin the process of change. It's important that we look at the different aspects of our lives because this is where our belief patterns play out: relationships, family, friendships, money, career, health, work/life balance. It's important that we ask ourselves, how are all these aspects of our lives working for us? If there is an area that needs work, or that we are unhappy about, it is necessary to look at how we think about it and what old beliefs may be holding us back. For example, maybe your work/life balance is causing you problems because you always seem to be working! You have a think about why that might be, and realise that you have always believed that hard work and long hours were essential to success. You remember hearing your father saying this (or maybe you don't know where you got this belief from), and you never questioned it for a moment. You put in the long hours, because you believed that this was necessary to have a successful career. I believed this myself until I heard my boss say, 'you need to work smart, not hard', and I thought to myself, *that's brilliant! I'll choose that belief instead!*

One area of my own life which has long challenged me is money. I not only grew up with lack and a strong belief in scarcity (learned from my parents and siblings), but also with a negative attitude about money itself. There were always rows in our home about money and I'd heard both parents saying that money was *the root of all evil*. I grew up hating money and thinking it *was* evil, so how could I possibly attract money to me! Changing my attitude about money and letting go of my fears around it has allowed me to become more prosperous. Money is a wonderful energy and can bring so much joy into our lives. We can use it to help others and the world around us – we can do so much good with it!

Examining our beliefs is like doing an inventory of our minds and can be really beneficial, especially when we consider that our minds are powerful tools with which we create our lives with every day. It is said that life is a self-fulfilling prophesy – we get back what we believe in – and I really believe this and have seen it play out in my own life. We need to learn how to get our minds working for us, through consciously choosing our thoughts to bring about the best results in our lives.

Practicing and teaching Reiki also helped me to feel more connected to the spiritual world and to understand the connection between my thinking, my emotions and my body. Whatever is going on in my mental body, and particularly in my emotional body, is definitely going on in my physical body. Looking back over my life, I have had various health problems, which I can now see were directly connected to how I was feeling and thinking at the time. I began to listen to my body and to what it was telling me and realised that my body had a language of its own. I began to notice stress because my shoulders would tighten or my hands would clasp. I noticed when I felt anger because my jaw would tighten or I would get a headache or sinus issues. Fear would manifest as a knot in my belly and the constant chest infections were definitely being caused by sadness and grief. My body is always informing me of what is really going on and I need to listen and pay attention at all times.

One day a friend, a reflexologist and herbalist who gave classes in well-being, asked me to give a talk to one of her groups about Reiki and holistic therapies. I was happy to oblige and really enjoyed giving the class. I felt so inspired afterwards that I decided to put together a six week course on personal development entitled 'Me, Myself and I,' and I sent it in to the local Education and Training Board. They contacted me soon after and I have been facilitating courses and workshops on personal development, relaxation and wellbeing, Reiki, meditation and mindfulness ever since. Mindfulness has become particularly popular in the last few years and I have really embraced it in my own life and feel passionately about it. For me, mindfulness is not a fad or the latest trend, it is so much more than that. Mindfulness brings solutions to the problems of the western world. We need to find ways and tools to quieten our busy minds, especially with our fast pace of life. We didn't know how to stop our minds from constantly thinking, constantly getting ahead of ourselves, regularly missing the moment entirely because of our rush to get to the next moment. All the while we are rushing through our days, weeks and years, ultimately rushing into an early grave. All of the inventions of the modern age – super-fast transport, washing machines, hoovers, dish-washers, etc. – promised to give us more time, and yet we have less time than ever! Mindfulness is about slowing down, pausing, connecting to the breath and the present moment. It's about stillness, meditation and learning to discipline the mind, which is new to us in the west as we do not have traditions of silence or meditation in our daily lives. Mindfulness is essentially about being at peace in each moment.

Bringing awareness to my body and to this moment (not thinking about the past or the future), accepting myself as I am and accepting my life as it is (without the need to judge it or fight it), brings peace to this moment, and ultimately to my life. This is what mindfulness is all about to me, and acceptance doesn't mean resignation or passivity – I don't have to like the present moment and I might want to change it, but I know that I need to love it, embrace it and accept it.

We all need to take time out every day to pause, to breathe, to empty our mind and to just 'be.' We need to stop rushing, stop creating stress in our lives and we need to learn how to recognise and let go of stress when we do feel it in our bodies and minds. We need to connect back in to our bodies and to our senses. 'Stop and smell the roses' is an old saying that has never been as relevant as it is today. We need to get the balance back in our lives and mindfulness is a great way to do that, offering wonderful tools to help us to improve the quality of our lives and to bring peace into every moment.

'Breath is the bridge which connects life to consciousness, which unites your body to your thoughts. Whenever your mind becomes scattered, use your breath as the means to take hold of your mind again.' Thich Nhat Hanh, *The Miracle of Mindfulness: An Introduction to the Practice of Meditation.*

Being positive, to me, is about always finding things to be grateful for. It's about looking for solutions, rather than focussing on problems. Positivity is about looking on the bright side, remembering to smile and laugh and not take life too seriously. It's about accepting that there will always be ups and downs and life can be so much easier when we learn to go with the flow and without judging or fight situations or events. Positivity is also about holding on to hope, when all else fails and not letting despair pull you down.

'Hope' is the thing with feathers

'Hope' is the thing with feathers –
That perches in the soul –
And sings the tune without the words –
And never stops – at all –

And sweetest – in the Gale – is heard –
And sore must be the storm –
That could abash the little Bird
That kept so many warm –

I've heard it in the chillest land –
And on the strangest Sea –
Yet – never – in Extremity,
It asked a crumb – of me.

– Emily Dickinson

Chapter 16

Sugar and Spice – Self-belief and the Joy of Life!

Through the process of counselling I gradually learned to love myself, I learned how to forgive others and then I learned to forgive myself. I've learned to follow my heart and be true to myself, after years of self-doubt. Following my heart hasn't always easy and has led to a lot of uncertainty, financial insecurity and changes of direction (the road less travelled!), but it has been so worth it. Yet it is only very recently that I have begun to believe in myself. I regularly said things like *fortune favours the brave*, and *what you put out comes back to you,* and have lived my life accordingly, but I began to wonder if it was ever going to work out for me, if I was ever going to have financial security doing what I love and what I'm passionate about. I kept moving forward, kept persevering, and when I doubted myself I always had the constant, unwavering light of absolute faith, from my mentor, Eileen Heneghan, who believed in me long before I ever believed in myself. And though it is still tentative, it is there nonetheless. I believe in myself, in my ability to be joyful, peaceful, healthy, creative, abundant and prosperous. I believe that I am realising my potential and my heart's desires every day. Every day I create my life through my thoughts and beliefs, my words, my actions and through my capacity to love, have compassion, empathy, understanding, forgiveness, tolerance, acceptance and patience. The old limited, lack-filled, fear-based life that I used to live has been transformed into an expansive, expressive, abundant, limitless life of love, connection and creativity.

So follow your dreams and your heart's desires and don't be afraid to dream big. We need the energy of passion to motivate us in times of struggle, so make sure that you are passionate about what you do and believe in what you are doing. The self-belief (if you don't already have it) will come along the way. The practice of mindfulness and using positive affirmations every day has really helped me along the way. There were days when the bills piled high and I would go for a walk and spend the first twenty minutes (or however long it took) saying, 'I am abundant and prosperous in every way. I realise my heart's desires and my dreams become a reality.' I would say it and say it until I believed it and would then enjoy the rest of my walk in peace. Don't give up on your dreams – keep moving forward and allow your own unique journey to unfold before you every day.

Our Deepest Fear

Our deepest fear is not that we are inadequate. Our deepest fear is that we are powerful beyond measure. It is our light, not our darkness that most frightens us. We ask ourselves, who am I to be brilliant, gorgeous, talented, fabulous? Actually, who are you not to be? You are a child of God. Your playing small does not serve the world. There is

nothing enlightened about shrinking so that other
people won't feel insecure around you. We are all
meant to shine, as children do. We were born to
make manifest the glory of God that is within us.
It's not just in some of us; it's in everyone. And
as we let our own light shine, we unconsciously
give other people permission to do the same. As
we are liberated from our own fear, our presence
automatically liberates others.

– Marianne Williamson, from *A Return to Love*

Lastly, I would just like to talk about joy – the icing on the cake! When I finally let go of the last remnants of shame, guilt and self-blame, I began to feel joy flowing into my life. It was like feeling the warm rays of the sun after being kept in the shade for so long. What a wonderful feeling it is to feel spontaneous joy. It was amazing the first time I felt it and it has become an important and necessary part of my life. What I have learned, though, is that my default mode (the way I felt for years) was anything but happy and I found myself reverting back to old ways of being disconnected and uneasy in myself. This was, of course, my pain body, which I spoke about earlier This confused me for a while because I knew that I could feel positive and that I could be joyful – so why wasn't I always like this? And then I realised that I had to consciously choose to be joyful every day. I had to decide every morning to be joyful and say *today I choose to be happy,* or *today I choose joy.* It isn't always easy and there are days when I fall well short of joyful or happy, but setting the intention every morning is a powerful and effective exercise.

I get it right far more often than wrong and it reminds me what my intention is for my life. If I find that something is getting in the way of joy, I will actively work on whatever is blocking me, so that I can walk in the sunshine once more!

Practicing gratitude every morning and every night really helps me to stay focussed on all the blessings that I have in my life, rather than focussing on what I don't have, or on what's missing (which is very easy in today's society). When we're always looking at what we don't have, or what we want next, we're never content. We're also focussing on 'the half-empty glass.' Remember that we get what we focus on, so we don't want to focus on nothing! Much better if we direct our energy to giving thanks for all we do have – and we can make that grow – because our gratitude is like water, light and food for the seeds that we sow in our lives.

I am convinced that God will only ask me one question when I reach the pearly gates and that is: 'Did you enjoy your life?' Because for me, I know that it is not enough that I survived my childhood, or that I lived to tell the tale. It will have been for nothing if I didn't learn to enjoy my life and my experiences. Life is a gift after all, and gifts are meant to be enjoyed. It is too precious for anything less. That's what I have learned so far. I'm hoping I have a way to go yet!

> *I can of mine own self, do nothing.*
> *Love thy neighbour, as thyself.*
> – Jesus

> *Kindness is a mark of faith, and whoever hath not kindness hath not faith.*
> – Mohammad

You can search throughout the entire universe for someone who is more deserving of your love and affection than you are yourself, and that person is not to be found anywhere. You, yourself, as much as anybody in the entire universe, deserve your love and affection.
– Buddha

Teach this triple truth to all: A generous heart, kind speech, and a life of service and compassion are the things which renew humanity.
– Buddha

God has no religion.
The one religion is beyond all speech.
– Mahatma Gandhi

The little space within the heart is as great as the vast universe. The heavens and the earth are there, and the sun and the moon and the stars. Fire and lightening and winds are there, and all that now is and all that is not.
– Swami Vivekananda

The moment I have realized God sitting in the temple of every human body, the moment I stand in reverence before every human being and see God in him – that moment I am free from bondage, everything that binds vanishes, and I am free.
– Swami Vivekananda

Love is the essence of God.
– Ralph Waldo Emerson

Afterword

We Need a Better Understanding of Child Sexual Abuse

We need to talk about child sexual abuse, because people aren't talking about it, even though one in four people have been victims of it. I believe one of the reasons is because most abusers are known to their victims and are often trusted members of their family or community. Abuse thrives on secrecy, shame and denial, and in order for this cycle of abuse and hurt to end we, as a society, must be willing to talk about it. No, it's not very savoury and nobody likes looking into the darkness that exists within us or those around us. It is so much easier to pretend that these things don't happen. Some of us bury the secrets so deeply that the memories of abuse never come to the surface – only our lives tell the story as we play out the unhappiness within us.

Sometimes a big event in our own life can trigger old memories of early childhood trauma. For example, it is quite common after childbirth, or if someone hears a similar story, to suddenly recall something, or have a flashback of a past event. When we become aware that the abuse has happened, we often don't know how to deal with it, or how to heal it. If we're lucky, we can begin the long healing process of understanding, forgiveness and self-love. I say lucky, because unfortunately this is not always the case. I have seen people blame themselves, after realising that they had been sexually abused as children. They are therefore unable to begin to heal, as they are too busy punishing themselves, usually through addiction or self-harming. It saddens me deeply when victims of child abuse continue to abuse themselves, long after their abuser has finished with them. We cannot help what has happened to us as children, but we can, hopefully, help ourselves as adults.

Paedophiles, to most of us, are evil people who prey on children. It has been easy to set them aside from society in general as most public cases of abuse have involved priests or people who the media have portrayed as social outcasts. Let's for a moment just think of the instances of abuse within the Catholic Church. Undoubtedly, there was a huge abuse of power and position within our communities. There was also a huge amount of hurt, guilt and confusion for the victims involved. Many injustices followed, by the poor handling of so many cases and, more importantly, there was a lot of unnecessary hurt through denial, secrecy and a lack of responsibility and courage.

It is also important to note that the sexual abuse of children in mainstream society has only very recently been spoken about in any public forum, anywhere in the world. Had the Church been more convinced of its parishioners' (and of society's) ability to cope with this issue in a positive and compassionate way, it may have spoken out sooner. The truth is that nobody was talking about child sexual abuse. Even when people were aware that abuse that was going on within their family or community, often nothing was done. It is important to remember that priests were all once members of families where, in many cases, abuse existed in some form or other. The horrible truth is that most abusers were once victims of abuse themselves and abuse often centres around the need to recover their own lost power. That is not to say that all abusers go on to abuse others, as this is clearly not the case. But what is crucial now is that we break the cycle of abuse and create a space for listening and healing.

Our responsibility is to stop being afraid and to stop distancing ourselves, or denying the existence of abuse within the family or community where it usually starts. *The SAVI Report*, published in 2002, yielded some surprising results, which have rarely been spoken about. One in five women (20.4 per cent) and one in six men (16.2 per cent) surveyed reported experiencing contact sexual abuse in childhood. Of these cases, a quarter (24 per cent) of girls and 14 per cent of boys surveyed were abused by a family member. Clerical/religious ministers or teachers constituted 3.2 per cent of all abusers. Fathers constituted 2.5 per cent of all abusers, with uncles (6.2 per cent), cousins (4.4 per cent) and brothers (3.7 per cent) among the most common other perpetrators. Why is it that as a society we could acknowledge, condemn, judge and openly discuss the 3.2 per cent that were clerics and we're still hardly talking about all of the other perpetrators? When I spoke to Elena O'Malley Dunlop (the then Chairperson of the Rape Crisis Centre), she called it 'the white elephant in the room.'

Unfortunately, *The SAVI Report* is the only study of its nature undertaken in Ireland to date. Further research carried out on the Rape Crisis Centre's website indicated that in 1997, there were 3,185 calls to the Dublin rape crisis centre. In 2000, there were 8,150 calls. In 2003, there were 11,863, and in 2006, there were 15, 781 calls made to the centre. Of these calls, over 40 per cent related to the sexual abuse of children. To be more precise: in 2006, 42.3 per cent of the 15,781 calls made related to children. That is a total of 6,675 calls made by adult survivors of abuse who are looking for help, often many years after the abuse has happened.

Here are a few more statistics from other countries:

- United States – adult retrospective studies show 1 in 4 women and 1 in 6 men were sexually abused by the age of 18. This gives a figure of 42 million survivors, according to the U.S. Department of Health.

- UK – a quarter of a million Britons are paedophiles. Of the 4.8 per cent of children abused, 90 per cent were by someone they knew (NSPCC).

- South Africa – a child is raped in South Africa every three minutes, according to a 2009 survey by Solidarity Helping Hand.

- India – in 2007, 53 per cent of children in India were victims of sexual abuse. This figure is now believed to be of epidemic proportions.

While these figures are shocking, they have helped reiterate to me how important it is to talk about child sexual abuse and find ways to stop it. We need to look at the bigger picture here. What we need to focus on is the provision of healing, for both victims and abusers. Society needs to be protected from abusers who are in denial and who do not want help – at whatever cost. At the same time, we need to stop judging and blaming and we need to listen. We need to show more understanding and compassion. In essence, we need to create a society where, firstly, crime is punished, and with very clear boundaries about what is a criminal offence with regard to child sexual abuse and ensure appropriate sentencing. Secondly, we need to listen, understand and provide support, rehabilitation and counselling where it is wanted and needed. Can you imagine how much someone must hate and loathe themselves for hurting a child in any way? How much confusion, shame, guilt and self-loathing they must have in their own lives? It's too easy to call people monsters, to create separation to make ourselves feel better, but we have seen from the past that this doesn't work. We need to find a new way.

Child sexual abuse exists in families and communities everywhere, in all levels of society, and we need to start talking about it. We need to be willing to understand the confusion, hurt, anger, guilt and shame children of abuse feel and how, if unhealed, these feelings impact hugely on the life of the adult victim. As noted earlier, most abused children fall into abusive adult relationships and often find intimate relationships impossible to maintain. Sexual promiscuity is another symptom of abuse, as are addictions to alcohol, cigarettes, food, narcotics, pornography and gambling. There is often confusion around sexuality, as the healthy boundaries that are a part of a child's normal development have been broken-down or eroded completely. There is a lot of self-loathing, low self-esteem and low confidence. Adult victims of abuse have a great deal of fear: fear of being abandoned, fear of being alone, fear of other people's anger, fear of being powerless, fear of feeling their feelings and many others.

Growing up in an alcoholic home, or in a physically violent home, usually has a similar impact on a child's self-esteem and confidence. Adult victims can also be left struggling to provide for themselves financially, as they usually believe that they don't deserve success or abundance and are often just trying to survive day by day.

It is important to say too that I have met many adults who are in pain because they were neglected emotionally as children, by one or both parents, or perhaps had a very controlling and domineering parent. This hurt and sadness can be very profound and is perfectly natural. It is not necessary to have been abused physically or sexually to feel pain, loss, grief, sadness, fear, anger from our childhood, or to feel the need to heal the hurt child inside.

But the emotional pain that is caused by an unhappy home, dysfunction and/or trauma in childhood needs to be healed. Avoiding the pain that we carry inside us can lead to destructive behaviour and addictions – of which there are many in society today. Someone with unresolved emotional pain is much more likely to become an addict and self-medicate their pain, often not knowing what else to do. A lot of victims of child sexual abuse, not surprisingly, become addicts too. They are also much more likely to suffer from chronic pain conditions in later life.

The healing process begins by acknowledging and working through the fears and the many emotions that are experienced, often with a professional psychologist or counsellor. For me, it was a roller coaster voyage of self-exploration and discovery, which led to understanding, awareness, acceptance and letting go. Sometimes the process was challenging and painful, other times magical and joyful.

Emptying out the closet of all my skeletons ultimately brought me such freedom and peace in my life. To have no secrets anymore was like being in the world with the sun shining over my head, instead of the big, grey cloud that had always been there. Ultimately, I learned over time to love and accept myself as I am, and to trust in myself.

> *When part of ourselves – the part we are ashamed of – is hidden, it can cause us problems, for what we hide from ourselves is a sort of enemy within. However, if we look straight at that part of ourselves, if we understand it and embrace it, we can turn it into a gift. Facing up to our shadow side forces us to acknowledge that nothing is all black or white, but that everything is made up of shades of grey. We can look at the wider context, at groups, communities, neighbourhoods, nations in the same way. On their own they are not all good or bad. They are a mixture, and no one of them is the cause of all the evil in the community or in the world. Good and evil are in all our hearts, and it is only when we acknowledge that, do we carry our responsibility for the good and evil in society.*

> *If only there were evil people somewhere insidiously committing evil deeds and it were necessary only to separate them from the rest of us and destroy them. But the line dividing good and evil cuts through the heart of every human being.*

> – Aleksandr Solzhenitsyn

List of Counselling Services

- Rape Crisis Centre (24 hour): 1800778888.
- CARI (Children at Risk in Ireland): 1890924567.
- NOVA (specifically for institutional abuse): 1800252524.
- One in Four (by appointment only): (01) 6624070.
- Tusla: check out Tusla.ie for a full listing of social workers in your area: (01) 7718500.

HSE Counselling Services

- Dublin – North of the Liffey: 1800234110.
- Kildare, South West Dublin (Tallaght, Walkinstown, Drimnagh, Crumlin, Clondalkin, Lucan), parts of Wicklow (e.g. Blessington, Baltinglass): 1800234112.
- Dublin – South of the Liffey (Ringsend-Crumlin), Dun Laoghaire etc., Wicklow: 1800234111.
- Laois, Longford, Offaly, Westmeath: 1800234113.
- Clare, Limerick, North Tipperary: 1800234115.
- Donegal, Sligo, Leitrim: 1800234119.
- Waterford, Kilkenny, Wexford, South Tipperary: 1800234118.
- Galway, Roscommon, Mayo: 1800234114.
- Cork, Kerry: 1800234116.
- Cavan, Monaghan, Meath, Louth: 1800234117.